Series Editor **Mike Burghall**

The *Resourceful* English Teacher

A complete teaching companion

Jon Chandler
Mark Stone

DELTA
PUBLISHING

Published by
DELTA PUBLISHING
Quince Cottage
Hoe Lane
Peaslake
Surrey GU5 9SW
England

© Jon Chandler and Mark Stone 1999

First published 1999
Reprinted with modifications 2003
Reprinted 2006
Reprinted 2009

ISBN 0 953 30981 9

All rights reserved. No part of this publication may be
reproduced, stored in a retrieval system, or transmitted,
in any form by any means, electronic, mechanical,
photocopying, recording, or otherwise, without the prior
permission of the publishers.

Designed by Trevor Sylvester (TSGD) and Christine Cox
Printed by Halstan & Co. Ltd., Amersham, Bucks., England

Acknowledgements
The publishers would like to thank Roger Hunt and
Helen Naylor. They are also grateful to Tanya Whatling
for her editorial help.

Author acknowledgements
Thanks to colleagues in our present and previous schools:
the Eckersley School of English, St Clare's, Oxford, and
above all the Swan School, for their support, advice and
constant inspiration.

For Teresa and Jacqueline

Foreword

This is, in many ways, the book that we would like to have been able to have to hand ourselves – both as inexperienced teachers starting our first jobs and as more experienced teachers looking for fresh inspiration.

Rather than focusing on one resource area, as is often the case, **The *Resourceful* English Teacher** addresses the full breadth of resources available to the language teacher, and offers a wide variety of activities and techniques for the modern classroom.

This book aims to be a resource in itself, presenting stimulating options and alternatives but without prescribing a specific approach to teaching. It can be 'dipped into' for a new way of recycling vocabulary, for example, or it can be read at greater length in order to get a fresh perspective on using, say, newspapers or the OHP.

We hope that these pages will be well-thumbed and the activities will be tried, played with and modified, to suit you and your classes – and that as a result you will feel refreshed, and the experience of being in your classroom will be richer, for both you and your students.

In short, we hope that it will enable you to become a more resourceful English teacher.

Jon Chandler
Mark Stone

Contents

Introduction

Today's language classroom is a complex and varied place. The demands made on the language teacher are no less challenging.

On the one hand, you may be in a position where all current technology is at your disposal (computer, video, internet). On the other hand, you may find yourself in a place where even a blackboard would be a luxury.

In both cases, you are required to be **resourceful**. This book is designed to help you in either of these circumstances, or as is more than probable, in any of the variety of situations that lie between.

Using This Book

The *Resourceful* **English Teacher** has been written to be useful to a wide variety of teachers of English.

- **For the less experienced teacher**, there is a wealth of ideas to help you build up a repertoire of activities in the classroom.

- **For the more experienced teacher**, some of the ideas in the book may already be familiar, although, even with the tried and tested activity, we have attempted to find a new twist. However, most will be new and will help you to see the resources available to you in a new light.

- **For the teacher trainer**, there is a wide range of materials to help you plan sessions on individual areas of classroom technique.

Planning Your Lessons

The *Resourceful* **English Teacher** is **not** a book of lesson plans but of activities, strategies and games, designed to help you exploit the resources and tools around you, **whatever they are**.

- Students enjoy **songs** but, in fact, rarely want to sing them. What else can you do?

- Low level students find **video** daunting. What kinds of tasks can bridge the gap?

- How can you use the **OHP** to create an interactive grammar game?

- What do you do with a **radio** in a classroom?

As this is not a book of lesson plans, you can be flexible in the way you use the activities. They can be used within a range of different lesson formats and at different stages of the course.

- A **filler** may come at the beginning of a lesson, to liven up students, in the middle, to indicate a change of pace or focus, or at the end, to fill an awkward gap.

- A **circle game** might be used to find out what students know or to practise what you have already taught them ... or both.

- An **icebreaker** can be used at the beginning of a course or as a way of clearing the air after an exam.

Planning Your Course

If you work with a coursebook you may be looking for ways of bringing in authentic materials either to augment a unit or to replace materials that are less relevant to your students' interests or needs. If this is the case, the Sections on *Newspapers, Articles* and *Songs* will give you the ideas you need to do this with confidence.

Alternatively, you may wish to use existing course material but in a different way that will bring it to life for your class.

- **Dialogues** can be presented in a variety of ways and then practised in order to memorise phrases or work on stress, rhythm and intonation.

- Grammar can be practised out loud using **circle games**.

- Personalised speaking tasks can be turned into **questionnaires** for students who are reluctant to voice their opinions spontaneously.

A number of activities in his book work well as 'threads' throughout a course. This means that you can use them on a regular basis, perhaps once or twice a week to give coherence and structure to a series of lessons. As students become more familiar with the activities, they will begin to use them more efficiently as the need to explain the 'hows' and the 'whys' of the game diminish.

- **Word box** activities can be used to build you students' active vocabularies over the course.

- **Articles** activities can help to establish strategies that students can use when reading on their own.

- A **circle game** can be played several times. Each time you can 'stir in' more language, making it more challenging.

Finding Your Way

The two hundred activities of **The *Resourceful English Teacher*** have been designed to be as accessible and easy to use as possible.

Sections

The book has been organised into Sections, each of which focuses on a particular resource. You will find a very brief explanation of each resource on the *Contents* pages.

Activities

Each Activity has been given a short and, we hope, memorable title followed by a brief description of the main aim and a set of procedures that can be taken in at a glance.

Headings

A series of Headings indicates everything you need to know to carry out each activity successfully.

Levels

We have suggested what we consider the optimum level, or range of levels, for each activity. These are described as: beginner, elementary, pre-intermediate, intermediate, upper-intermediate and advanced.

Activity types

We indicate whether students will be working in pairs or groups; if this is suggested as an option, then the activity can also be organised for the class as a whole. If there is a competitive element, or if the students need to be able to move around, then this too is indicated.

Equipment / Materials

Here are listed the things you will need to have with you in the classroom.

Plus ...

Here you will find any specific materials that you will need to find, or to prepare, and on which the activity is based.

Appendix

Suggested material for some of the activities from the *Circles* section is provided in a separate Appendix at the back of the book.

1

Newspapers

Newspapers are a valuable but often under-used classroom resource. There is a breadth of coverage in them, which means there is something of interest to almost all readers. They provide a good source of popular culture, as they often include articles on pop music, TV and sport, as well as advertisements for products and events. One newspaper may be the source of a wide range of activities, for all levels.

Many teachers are afraid that their students might be intimidated by English language newspapers. In this section, however, we offer a range of activities which acquaint students with newspapers through appropriate tasks for their level of English.

You may wish to consider which English-speaking countries your students identify with most positively. Very often this identification conveniently coincides with the availability of newspapers, but it is worth remembering that most newspapers can be obtained from their publishers by post.

Describe a Typical Reader

Use newspapers to stimulate your students' curiosity about English-speaking cultures

Level	Elementary onwards
Activity type	Groupwork
Equipment/ Materials	None
Plus ...	Three or four different English language newspapers

- Put the students into small groups.

- Give each group a different newspaper and the name of a typical person who might read this newspaper. The aim for each group is to use any clues in the newspaper to help write a description of this typical reader.

- At lower levels, brainstorm any questions one might ask about a person, for example 'What does he look like?' 'What's her taste in clothes?' and write these on the board.

- In groups, students try to answer these questions in order to build up a picture of their imaginary reader.

- Students then present the description of their typical reader to the class.

- At higher levels this activity could be used as an introduction to a wider discussion of class and politics in modern Britain, the USA or wherever.

Ailing Newspaper

A challenging task which puts your students at the heart of Fleet Street

Level	Intermediate onwards
Activity type	Groupwork
Equipment/ Materials	None
Plus ...	Two different English language newspapers (see below)

- Put the students into groups and give out copies of two rival newspapers. Suggestions for UK newspapers are *The Independent* and *The Times, The Guardian* and *The Independent, The Times* and *The Daily Telegraph.*

- Tell the students that they are to decide which of the two newspapers has the higher circulation. The students decide in their groups which newspaper they think sells the most copies per month and why. They then tell the class, justifying their views.

- Reveal the truth (*The Daily Telegraph* 946,697; *The Times* 671,340; *The Guardian* 409,569; *The Independent* 221,926, as at March 2003).

- Then tell the students that they are working as consultants to the newspaper with the lower circulation. In groups, they should suggest different business plans that will revive that particular newspaper's circulation.

- After a short time the groups can present their plans to the class. At the end, the class vote for the plan that they feel is most likely to succeed.

Preconceptions

How well do your students know British and American people? Help them to find out

Level	Pre-intermediate onwards
Activity type	Pairwork/groupwork (optional)
Equipment/ Materials	None
Plus ...	Two or three British and American newspapers

- Put the students into pairs or small groups and ask the students to write down a number of generalisations concerning British and American people that they themselves might feel to be true, for example 'Americans are more concerned with money, the British with class.'

- Once students have completed their lists, circulate British and American newspapers among the pairs/groups, and the students should search the newspapers for evidence to prove or refute their assertions. If at the initial stage the groups can only suggest a few generalisations, you may wish to pool these, by writing them on the board, before going on to the next stage.

- Once all the newspapers have been circulated, each group should make a presentation in which they tell the class which generalisations have been confirmed, and which have been disproved, giving their reasons as they go along.

Present a Newspaper

Learn about the differences between newspapers – and practise a good deal of vocabulary as well

Level	Elementary to Intermediate
Activity type	Groupwork
Equipment/ Materials	None
Plus ...	One different newspaper for every three or four students in the class

- Pre-teach any essential newspaper vocabulary, for example *column, article, feature, caption, headline.*

- Put the students into small groups and give each group a different newspaper.

- Tell them to analyse all the different sections of the newspaper to see how much column space is allocated to different topic areas and how much advertising there is.

- The students then present the description of the newspaper that they have been examining to the class.

Newspaper Cultures

Use a 'pyramid' discussion (see below) to discover the differences between two cultures as exemplified in their newspapers

Level	Elementary onwards
Activity type	Groupwork
Equipment/ Materials	None
Plus ...	Copy/copies of an English language newspaper and of a first language newspaper

- Pre-teach any essential newspaper vocabulary, for example *column, article, feature, caption, headline.*

- Put the students into small groups of a maximum of six students. Give each of these groups an English language newspaper and a first language newspaper for a similar readership, for example *The Times* and *El País.*

- Divide the group into two, so that half of the group looks at *The Times*. The others study *El País*. They should analyse all the different sections of their newspaper to see how much column space is allocated to different topic areas.

- Students then work together within the larger group to produce sentences comparing the two newspapers, for example: 'There are more sports pages in *The Times* than in *El País.*'

- Pool the observations by asking each group in turn to read out their sentences. Invite discussion on the possible differences between the two countries.

Newspaper Quiz

Use an element of competition to get your students reading newspapers

Level	Elementary onwards
Activity type	Groupwork
Equipment/ Materials	Photocopies
Plus ...	Multiple copies of a single newspaper

- Prepare a written quiz, the length and difficulty of which will depend on the level of your class.

- Questions may be open and aim to stimulate discussion, for example, 'What would you watch on Thursday night and why?' or closed with right/wrong answers, for example: 'What was the temperature in Athens yesterday?'

- Put the students into groups and set the quiz.

- Discuss the answers.

Where Are The Correspondents?

Excellent practice for finding one's way around a newspaper and scanning

Level	Beginner and Elementary
Activity type	Pairwork/groupwork (optional)
Equipment/ Materials	Photocopies
Plus ...	A copy of a different English language newspaper and a photocopied map of the world for each pair/group of students

- Put the students into pairs or small groups.

- Give each pair/group a photocopied map of the world and a different newspaper (serious newspapers generally work better for this activity).

- Tell them that each newspaper has correspondents in different parts of the world; their task is to mark on their map the location of all the correspondents for the newspaper that they have been given.

- At the end of the activity, all the maps and newspapers can be compared.

Article Pairing

Persuade your students to use their armoury of reading skills

Level	Pre-intermediate onwards
Activity type	Groupwork
Equipment/ Materials	None
Plus ...	One copy of two different newspapers for each group

- Put the students into groups and give each group two different newspapers, preferably a quality newspaper and a tabloid.

- Ask each group to draw up a list of articles on the same subject in each newspaper, for example, different reports of the same crime, conflicting reviews of the same film. Students need not read all the articles in their entirety, but merely enough of each article to be able to identify its subject.

- Extend the activity by encouraging the students to present their findings to the class.

Headline 'Call My Bluff'

A panel game already used in English language classrooms with individual words, but not as yet with newspaper headlines

Level	Intermediate onwards
Activity type	Competitive activity/game
Equipment/ Materials	None
Plus ...	A range of newspaper articles (see below)

- Divide the class into groups or teams, and give each team two or three articles with ambiguous headlines, for example, 'Soap Opera Star Still in Closet' or 'Schools Place Emphasis on Tables' (You will need twelve different articles if there are four teams.)

- Each team should make up three alternative stories that could equally well accompany these headlines.

- The game starts. Each team presents their headline along with the three invented stories and the original story.

- The other teams decide which of the four stories they have just heard is the most plausible. Award points accordingly.

Chequebook Journalism

The newshounds have sniffed out some good stories – can they sell them for a good price?

Level	Intermediate onwards
Activity type	Mingle/open space activity
Equipment/ Materials	None
Plus ...	Brief news stories from English language newspapers (see below)

- Cut out individual short news stories from a newspaper - the 'News in Brief' section of *The Guardian* is one good source.

- Divide the class into 'journalists' and 'editors.' Assign the editors a newspaper and give the journalists a story each.

- The journalists aim to sell their story to the highest bidder. They have to think of different arguments that will persuade the editors of each newspaper to buy their story.

- The editors have a limited budget, but are all keen to increase their readership.

- At the end of the activity the editors tell the class which stories they have bought and give their reasons.

Pushy Paparazzi

Sell pictures and learn English

Level	Elementary onwards
Activity type	Mingle/open space activity
Equipment/ Materials	None
Plus ...	Newspaper photographs (see below)

- Cut out some typical paparazzi shots, for example Jennifer López in a low-cut dress or Brad Pitt without his shirt.

- Divide the class into 'editors' and 'photographers.'

- The photographers should try to sell their photographs to the editors for the highest price.

- Encourage fierce competition!

Spot the Paper

See how much your students have learned about English language newspapers

Level	Intermediate onwards
Activity type	Groupwork; competitive activity (optional)
Equipment/ Materials	Photocopies
Plus ...	Photocopies of four or five newspaper articles, each from a different newspaper

- Give your students a selection of perhaps five articles. You may wish to omit the headlines.

- Tell them to skim the articles and decide which British newspaper they are taken from, supporting their decision using their own knowledge of the press.

- Alternatively this can be played as a gambling game, the students who guess correctly winning token money, the others losing their original bets.

3

Articles

Many coursebooks contain articles, or parts of articles, from newspapers and magazines. Sometimes, these are graded to the students' level, but increasingly they remain as authentic material. Very often, 'real' articles are included along with appropriate activities, which dovetail with the book's grammatical and lexical syllabus.

Selecting your own articles from English language newspapers and magazines has additional advantages. Newspapers and magazines contain an enormous range of text types. Many subjects are covered in a variety of styles and registers, allowing you to choose something that suits both your students' needs and interests. Articles can be topical. Students can use their knowledge of current events as well as their own experience to help them understand what they are reading and this will help them become more confident.

Information Gap

Different newspapers often cover the same stories

Level	Elementary onwards
Activity type	Pairwork/groupwork
Equipment/ Materials	Photocopies
Plus ...	Two newspaper articles (see below) and a list of questions (see below)

- Choose two articles, both on the same subject, from two different newspapers. Before the lesson, produce a set of questions which fit any of the following categories:
(a) questions best answered using information from both the articles;
(b) questions eliciting different answers from the two articles;
(c) questions, the answers to which can only be found in one of the articles. Photocopy one copy of the set of questions, and one copy of each article, for each student.

- Put the class into two groups: group A and group B. Give each student in group A a copy of article A, and each student in group B a copy of article B. Ask the students to read the whole of their article individually at this stage.

- When the students have read their articles, they should, within their groups, resolve any vocabulary problems, first by discussion and then, if necessary, by using dictionaries.

- Hand out the questions. Working in AB pairs, students pool information and discuss differences in their answers.

Style and Register

Same story but look out for the differences in language

Level	Intermediate onwards
Activity type	Pairwork/groupwork
Equipment/ Materials	Photocopies
Plus ...	Two newspaper articles (see below) and a simple table (see below)

- Choose two articles from two newspapers, both on the same subject but differing in terms of style and register. Before the lesson, produce a table consisting of three vertical columns headed 'Information contained only in article A', 'Information contained only in article B', 'Information contained in articles A and B'. Photocopy one copy of this table, as well as a copy of each article, for each student.

- Put the class into two groups: group A and group B. Give each student in group A a copy of article A, and each student in group B a copy of article B. Ask the students to read the whole of their article individually and resolve any problems, either by discussion, within their group or by using a dictionary.

- At the end of this stage put students into AB pairs. Give each pair a table to fill in. When they have finished ask them to select four or five of the items that they have written in the column labelled 'Information in articles A and B'. Ask them to underline the phrases that express these items. Discuss the differences in language.

Collocation Prediction

Exploit newspapers in order to present and practise new collocations

Level	Intermediate onwards
Activity type	Pairwork/groupwork
Equipment/ Materials	Photocopies
Plus ...	A newspaper article (see below)

- Find a text which is rich in collocations. Political articles are good and full of such examples as 'hotly denied', 'flatly refused' or 'sweeping changes'.

- Take out ten collocations and type them as a list of individual words. Photocopy the list for each pair of students.

- In pairs students try to match the words in order to reproduce the ten collocations. Check their answers at this stage.

- Ask the students which current news story the collocations have been taken from. If they don't know, tell them. Ask the students to suggest any other phrases or vocabulary items that they think are likely to occur in the story and write these on the board.

- In pairs or groups, the students include the original collocations, and any of the phrases agreed on, in order to create their own version of the original news story.

- The students then read the original newspaper article and compare it with their own version.

Headline Prediction

Maximize your students' curiosity before reading a newspaper article

Level	Pre-intermediate onwards
Activity type	Groupwork
Equipment/ Materials	OHP; photocopies
Plus ...	A newspaper article (see below)

- On an OHP, show the students the headline to an article. Students should try to predict what the article might be about.

- Once they have agreed on the actual subject of the article, put them into small groups and ask them to write ten questions that they would like the article to answer.

- You may wish to ask the students to write them on OHTs in order to compare them as a class.

- Students then read the article to see whether their own questions have been answered.

- In their groups, the students may then discuss likely answers to their remaining questions.

Obituaries

A roleplay with a difference

Level	Pre-intermediate onwards
Activity type	Groupwork; homework (optional)
Equipment/ Materials	Photocopies
Plus ...	Four or five obituaries and a sheet of paper with four or five names on it (see below)

- Collect four or five interesting obituaries. Photocopy one copy of each obituary for every student.

- Put the students into four or five groups. Give each group a different obituary to study.

- When they have fully understood the content of the article that they have been given, reseat the class into new groups. Each of these new groups should contain at least one student from each of the original groups.

- Each student takes it in turns to reminisce about their life and times. (Only allow reference to the text if essential.) The other students ask questions and sympathize.

- Give them time, once the activity is over to make notes, asking further questions if necessary. These notes can then be written up for homework.

Film Reviews

Everybody enjoys a good film

Level	Pre-intermediate onwards
Activity type	Groupwork
Equipment/ Materials	Photocopies
Plus ...	A selection of film reviews

- Select four or five reviews of current cinema releases. They should be similar in length. Photocopy one copy of each for every student.

- Put the class into groups of four or five (depending on the number of reviews you have). Give each student in each group a different film review. Allow the students time to read the reviews.

- Take back the reviews. Tell the students that each group is going out to see a film together; they have to decide which film they want to see. Students discuss the films and negotiate a plan for the evening.

- Each group then tells the class which film they have chosen and why.

- At lower levels, you may wish to group together the students who are reading the same review, before they meet the other students who have read a different review.

Day-by-Day Weather Reports

Everybody knows that the English always talk about the weather – prepare your students!

Level	Beginner to Pre-intermediate
Activity type	Whole class
Equipment/ Materials	OHP (optional); photocopies
Plus ...	A weather report

- Give the students a copy of a weather report/forecast (local, national or international) from the current day's newspaper, or make a photocopied OHT of the forecast, and present this.

- Study it as a class, focusing on the language used to describe the weather.

- Tell the students to look out of the window and talk about what the weather is like. Ask them if they think that the forecast will come true, and encourage them to make their own predictions about the weather. Make a record of these.

- The following day, talk about what the weather has been like. Compare the class's forecast with the one in the previous day's newspaper.

World Weather Reports

Widen your class's weather horizons

Level	Pre-intermediate onwards
Activity type	Whole class
Equipment/ Materials	Single VHS player + TV (optional); photocopies
Plus ...	A camcorder or a cassette-recorder (see below) and a copy of the world weather report

- Make a recording of the TV news weather report and make a copy of the 'Around the World' section of the current day's newspaper weather report for every two or three students.

- Show your students the video of the weather report and study the language used.

- Hand out the 'Around the World' photocopies and allocate a city to each student. Ask the students to prepare to give a brief weather report from their part of the world. Give them time to prepare this and help with any vocabulary; ask them to be imaginative.

- When you feel that your students are prepared, record them giving their individual weather reports.

- This activity works particularly well with a multilingual class presenting weather reports for their own countries.

Agony Aunts

Everybody loves giving advice – the question is, is it good enough?

Level	Pre-intermediate onwards
Activity type	Pairwork
Equipment/ Materials	Photocopies
Plus ...	A problem page from a magazine or newspaper

- Take a problem page that has a variety of problem letters and replies giving advice.

- Cut the page up, so that each letter and each reply is now separate.

- Paste these onto a piece of paper in a random order; however, omit three of the replies and photocopy these onto another piece of paper.

- Finally, photocopy both pasted up pages, one for each pair of students in the class.

- Hand out the photocopies with the letters and answers (but not the photocopy of the three replies) and ask each pair of students to match them. Explain that there are three letters that do not yet have any replies.

- Check the matching exercise as a class.

- Explain to the students that they are now working as 'agony aunts' for the same newspaper. Working in pairs, they are to write the replies to the three unanswered letters.

- When the students have finished their replies, put these up around the class and encourage them to read each other's.

- At the end of the lesson, hand out the real agony aunt replies for the students to compare with their own.

Scissors

Use newspaper articles to create a discourse puzzle

Level	Pre-intermediate onwards
Activity type	Pairwork
Equipment/ Materials	Photocopies
Plus ...	Two newspaper articles (see below)

- Take two articles on the same subject and from the same newspaper, but from two consecutive days. Ensure that the typeface in each article is the same.

- Photocopy one copy of each article for each pair of students.

- Cut up each copy of the article column by column, and then cut between each paragraph.

- Mix up the two articles, but make sure that you deal with only one copy of each article at a time.

- Put each pair of cut-up articles into an envelope. Don't forget to keep a copy of the complete versions.

- Divide your class into pairs and give each pair one of the envelopes. Ask them to piece the articles back together again.

Plagiarists

A text-completion task that focuses on register

Level	Intermediate onwards
Activity type	Pairwork
Equipment/ Materials	Photocopies
Plus ...	Two newspaper articles (see below)

- Choose two news articles reporting the same story, the first from a tabloid newspaper, and the second from a broadsheet.

- Photocopy both articles for the number of students in your class, but cut the broadsheet article into two after the second or third paragraph.

- Study the article from the tabloid newspaper with the class in any way that you wish to, paying particular attention to issues of register and style.

- Put your students into pairs. Give each pair the first section of the broadsheet article. Ask them to identify any differences in style between the two articles. Write these up on the board.

- Then ask the students to work in pairs to complete the second article. They should select any appropriate information from the first, but should attempt to reformulate it in a style and register more appropriate to the second newspaper.

- Finally, give each pair the copies of the rest of the second article.

TV Partners

Students probably do this in their spare time anyway!

Level	Beginner to Pre-intermediate
Activity type	Mingle; homework (optional)
Equipment/ Materials	Photocopies
Plus ...	A TV schedule from a newspaper and a simple table (see below)

- Photocopy the TV schedule for each pair of students. If you are working in the UK, try to use the TV schedule for that evening. If you are working abroad, try to include a TV schedule that includes some English language channels.

- Make a simple table with each hour, from six o'clock until midnight, marked on it. (You may wish to omit this stage and ask your students to make the table during the class.)

- Divide the students into pairs and give each pair the photocopied TV schedule, and the table if you have prepared it. The students decide individually what they wish to watch that evening. They have to watch TV continuously between six o'clock and midnight.

- Having filled in the form, the students then mingle to find their most compatible TV partner for the evening, asking questions like, 'I'm watching Blind Date. Are you?'

- As homework, you could ask the students to watch one English language programme that evening.

Couch Potatoes

Something of a challenge!

Level	Elementary to Intermediate
Activity type	Groupwork; homework (optional)
Equipment/ Materials	Photocopies
Plus ...	A TV schedule from a newspaper and a simple table (see below)

• Photocopy a TV schedule for the day and, if you wish, a table with the hours between six o'clock and midnight marked on it.

• Ask your students to read the TV schedule individually and to write down their preferred list of programmes for the evening. Tell them that they *must* spend the entire evening watching television.

• Put the students into groups of three or four and ask them to compare schedules.

• Now tell them that they all have to spend the evening watching TV **together** and that there is only one television in the house. In their groups they have to negotiate a compromise schedule which they all find acceptable.

• As homework, ask the students to watch one English language programme that evening.

'Peopling' the News

Reconstructing the news using the human resources at your disposal

Level	Intermediate onwards
Activity type	Groupwork/mingle
Equipment/ Materials	Photocopies
Plus ...	Newspaper article/s (see below) and a cassette-recorder or camcorder (optional)

• Find an interesting story in the news that has an important human-interest element and that involves a meeting between the characters in the story. Try the gossip columns of national dailies, local newspapers and gossip magazines such as *Hello!* or *OK!*

• Either study an article written about the story, or follow a series of articles as they appear over a few days.

• If you are using only one article, use an article which deals with a dramatic, and possibly emotional, meeting; peace talks are good examples. After studying the article and discussing the feelings of all involved, set up a roleplay in which the students re-enact the meeting they have just been reading about.

• If you are using a series of articles, use a story that leads up to a dramatic meeting. Follow the events leading up to the meeting, and then, on the day that the meeting itself is due to take place, set up a roleplay in which the students enact the meeting as they think it will happen.

• Compare the roleplay with what actually took place.

And Today's Article is ...

Unsure which article to read next?

Level	Pre-intermediate onwards
Activity type	Groupwork
Equipment/ Materials	None
Plus ...	Four or five short newspaper articles on a range of topics

• Divide the class into four or five groups. Give each group a different article.

• Tell the students to read their article alone, and then, working as a group, to produce a list of five reasons why the rest of the class should read the article. Give them a time limit.

• Each group takes it in turn to persuade the class as a whole that their article is the most interesting.

• The class votes to decide which article they would like to look at.

• As homework you can give students the second most popular article.

3

Songs

Students often come into the classroom humming songs to which they don't know the words. Knowing the words gives many teenagers kudos, a greater insight into the minds of their idols, and may even help with language acquisition. Teachers do not often have so much curiosity available in the classroom.

For learners, as indeed for native-speakers, the main desire is to understand the song, not necessarily the details, but at least the gist. Non-native speakers often find English language songs particularly daunting and frustrating. What is important, though, is the relationship between the material and the task that is set.

The activities in this section help students to understand the songs, and in the process, develop their English in terms of grammar, vocabulary and pronunciation.

Songs can often be bought cheaply in compilations. Students may have their own collections of English songs, and they appreciate it when the teacher borrows one of their songs and develops a lesson around it.

Many songs now come with a video. Exploit this relationship. You may also find the techniques in the *TV and Video* chapter of this book useful with songs.

Line-by-Line Mingle

Students mingle to unmuddle a song

Level	Beginner to Intermediate
Activity type	Mingle/open space activity
Equipment/ Materials	Single cassette player; photocopies
Plus ...	A recording of a song and a cut-up text (see below)

- Photocopy the words of a song and cut up the song line by line.

- Give each line to a different student. (If you have too many students for the lines of the song, you may have to allocate two students to a line.)

- Ask the students to stand up.

- Then ask them to stand in a line in the correct sequence, in order to form the lines of the song, in the correct order.

- When the students have finished jostling for position, play the song, and see if the students want to move. You may need to do this more than once.

- Once the lines are in order, students should read the song aloud, saying one line each. They could even sing it, but don't count on it!

Every Breath You Fake ...

Shake, take, slake, rake - how many rhymes for '-ake' can your students think of?

Level	Pre-intermediate onwards
Activity type	Mingle; groupwork/pairwork (optional)
Equipment/ Materials	Single cassette player; photocopies
Plus ...	Teacher's knowledge of phonemic chart; a recording of a song and the words (see below)

- Choose a song, preferably with multiple rhymes; 'rap' is excellent for this. Put a gap at the end of each line of the lyrics, and make one copy for each student.

text

Every breath you _____
Every move you _____

- At the top of a small poster, write the phonemic transcription for the ending of one of the words that you have omitted. Repeat this for each group of line endings.

poster

/eɪk/

- Divide your class into pairs and circulate the posters. The students have to write on the posters all the words they can think of which end with the sound that has been indicated.

- Put the posters up around the room, and give the students the gapped text of the song. They should circulate, trying to complete the gaps in their texts by selecting the words from the posters.

- Finally, play the song to check the answers.

Where Are all the Nouns?

An alternative to the standard gap-fill

Level	Elementary onwards
Activity type	Pairwork/groupwork
Equipment/ Materials	Single cassette player; photocopies
Plus ...	A recording of a song and the words (see below)

- Type up the song, omitting words belonging to one grammatical category, for example nouns, verbs, or adjectives. Do not indicate **where** these words have been omitted.

- Put the students into pairs, and give each pair the text. Ask them to put a cross wherever they think a word is missing.

- Check together as a class.

- Now working in small groups the students then brainstorm possible words for the gaps.

- Play the song and check the answers. Discuss which of the alternatives that the students have created might be possible in the context of the song and how these alternatives might change the meaning.

Wrong Words in Text

Old MacDonald had a pram

Level	All levels
Activity type	Pairwork/groupwork (optional)
Equipment/ Materials	Single cassette player; Photocopies
Plus ...	A recording of a song and the words (see below)

- Type up a song such as 'Old MacDonald had a farm', putting in wrong, possibly hilarious, 'mistakes' into the text, for example 'Old MacDonald had a *pram*'.

- The students read the text, working in pairs or small groups, and try to spot the mistakes and correct them.

- Play the song to check the answers.

Picture Gaps

... and on that farm he had a ...

Level	Beginner and Elementary
Activity type	Whole class
Equipment/ Materials	Single cassette player; photocopies
Plus ...	A recording of a song and the words (see below)

- Type up a song such as 'Old MacDonald had a farm', replacing the target vocabulary with small pictures, for example:

- Play the song and ask the students to sing along with it.

- At the end, ask them to write down the words next to each picture.

Jumbled Words

Old farm a MacDonald had

Level	Beginner to Intermediate
Activity type	Pairwork
Equipment/ Materials	Single cassette player; photocopies
Plus ...	A recording of a song and the words (see below)

- Type up a song such as 'Old MacDonald had a farm' with the words in some of the lines put into the wrong order. Make a copy for each pair of students.

- Put the students into pairs and give out the copies.

- Students work together to put the words into the correct order within the lines.

- Play the song to check the answers.

Singogloss

A challenging variation on the dictogloss idea

Level	Elementary onwards
Activity type	Pairwork/groupwork (optional)
Equipment/ Materials	Single cassette player; photocopies
Plus ...	A recording of a song and the words

- Choose a song, preferably one that tells a story. Make one copy of the words for each student.

- Play the song through once. Ask the students one or two questions about it.

- Tell them that you are going to play it again, pausing briefly at the end of each verse. They are to write down any important words or phrases they hear – they are not expected to write down all of it.

- Play it again.

- In pairs or small groups, they pool their notes and then construct a text based on their notes.

- Finally, compare their texts to the original song lyrics.

Song Dictation

Mind the gap!

Level	Elementary onwards
Activity type	Pairwork/groupwork (optional)
Equipment/ Materials	Single cassette player; photocopies
Plus ...	A recording of a song and the words (see below)

- Choose a slow song with clear words. Good examples are *Play with Fire* (Rolling Stones) and *Yellow* (Coldplay). Make a copy for each student in the class.

- Give each student a blank piece of paper, or alternatively, a copy of the song with a line indicating every missing word in the song.

- Play the song, if necessary pausing at the end of each line or verse, and ask the students to write it down as a dictation.

- Repeat as often as the students feel they need it. After listening to the song each time, they compare their texts with their partner's.

- Finally, hand out the copies of the full text for the students to check.

Split Song

A listening activity where the students have all the answers

Level	All levels
Activity type	Pairwork
Equipment/ Materials	Single cassette player; photocopies
Plus ...	A recording of a song and the words (see below)

- Choose a song and type it up. Make two copies, one with the odd numbered lines gapped and the even numbered lines complete (copy A), and the other with the even numbered lines gapped and the odd numbered lines complete (copy B). Make one copy of either A or B for each student.

- Play the song through once. Ask students one or two questions about it.

- Split the class into pairs, giving one member of each pair copy A, and the other copy B. Play the song again, pausing every few lines. Ask the students to complete the gapped lines individually.

- When the dictation is finished, students check the answers with their partners.

Running Dictation

'Run rabbit, run'

Level	Elementary onwards
Activity type	Competitive activity/game
Equipment/ Materials	Single cassette player; photocopies
Plus ...	A recording of a song and the words (see below)

- Make one copy of the words of the song: *Run rabbit, run rabbit, run, run, run/Don't give the farmer his fun, fun, fun/He'll get by without his rabbit pie/So run rabbit, run rabbit, run, run, run* for each student, and one large copy, to be used as a poster.

- Play the song through once. Ask the students one or two questions about it.

- Place the poster of the song on a wall outside the classroom.

- Put the students into groups of three or four. One student in each group should act as a 'scribe', the others should take it in turns to act as 'runners'.

- The runners read the song placed outside the classroom. They memorize as large a fragment of the song as they can, return to the group as quickly as possible, and relay the text to the scribe, who then writes it down.

- The groups then race each other to see which group can transcribe the complete text of the song first.

- As soon as one group has finished, play the song and check the answers.

- Finally, give all the students a copy of the words to the song.

My Song

Get your students to talk about what they probably talk about outside class anyway!

Level	Elementary onwards
Activity type	Whole class
Equipment/ Materials	Single cassette player

- Ask your students to come in with their favourite song in English, and to be prepared to talk about it.

- They play the music to the class, and explain why it is important to them.

- Let the other students ask questions.

- This can be done, either as a single lesson, or as an ongoing series or 'thread' (see *Introduction*), through the term or course.

'A and R People'

Your class keep a look out for new talent

Level	Pre-intermediate onwards
Activity type	Groupwork
Equipment/ Materials	Single cassette player
Plus ...	Recordings of a variety of songs (see below)

- Choose a selection of songs which you think will be unknown to your students; they may be very recent, or they may be 'oldies'.

- Describe the role of Artist and Repertoire personnel in a modern record company (they select and market the bands).

- Put the class into groups. Tell the students that they are 'A and R people,' and that they are going to hear 'demo tapes' from some promising young bands.

- Play the first song. The students, working in their groups, discuss whether the band is worth 'signing', the sort of people the band might appeal to, and how the band should be presented to the public.

- Repeat this procedure for each song.

- To complete the session, if you have sufficient knowledge, tell the class how successful these bands have actually been.

4

Readers

Most of the major publishers now produce series of graded readers. They are very varied and include contemporary fiction, as well as classics and books of films. The wide range of titles means that it is relatively easy for a student to choose a book that fits their interests, or for a teacher to choose a class reader that will appeal to a given class.

The activities in this section fall into two parts: activities which can be used when the whole class is using a single reader; and activities to be used when students are able to select their own reader from the school library, a bookshop or a school-supported mailorder scheme.

These activities aim to motivate students to read, and to develop as independent learners. Initially, students will need to be supported through the reading process. This can be accomplished by dealing with problems of comprehension and vocabulary, setting realistic reading targets and providing appropriately challenging tasks. This will help to give students the confidence they need to read independently in their own time.

Activities in this section allow students to practise the skills of skimming, scanning, and deducing from context, as well as creating an opportunity for fluency practice. Students will also be able to extend their vocabulary and develop their writing skills.

The activities in the first part (*Using a Class Reader*) depend on the class having read to the same point in the reader. The activities in the second part (*Using Different Readers*) are designed for when students have chosen their own individual readers.

Comparing First Paragraphs

For those happy situations where you have a choice of more than one set of class readers for your students

Level	Elementary onwards
Activity type	Groupwork
Equipment/ Materials	None
Plus ...	Sets of class readers

- This activity, unlike those following, should be used *before* the class has started on a reader.

- Put the class into as many groups as you have sets of class readers.

- Give each group a different reader and ask them to look at it for a few minutes. They should examine the text on the back and read the first two or three paragraphs.

- Ask each group to 'present' its reader to the class. After all the presentations, the students vote to choose the class reader.

Group Questions

An activity that lives, or dies, on the quality of the questions

Level	Elementary onwards
Activity type	Groupwork
Equipment/ Materials	Photocopies
Plus ...	A set of class readers

- Write a series of questions on the reader so far.

- Put the students into groups and ask them to answer the questions as a group. Encourage lively discussion.

- Do this regularly. Each time, write questions that encourage the students to look at the book in a different way. Include closed questions to test comprehension and open questions to encourage the students to compare their own responses to the text.

- Frame the questions around a particular theme.

- One week, write questions which examine the moral dilemmas faced by the characters: the decisions they have made, and the decisions they could/should have made.

- The following week, write questions which examine alternative possibilities within the plot. Your choice of theme will give the students practice in particular grammatical areas, for example in the above, modality and conditionals.

Passage Questions

It's amazing how motivating it is to make questions to test somebody else

Level	Elementary onwards
Activity type	Groupwork
Equipment/ Materials	Photocopies
Plus ...	A set of class readers

- Choose two or more unconnected, but significant, passages from the chapters that the class has read so far. Photocopy them, on separate pieces of paper, one for each student in the class.

- Split the class into groups (two or more, depending on the size of your class) and give each group one of the passages.

- Each group works together, reading their own passage, and discussing its place in the story so far. They resolve any problems of vocabulary within the passage as they go along.

- Tell each group to produce a list of questions on this passage for the other group. They may refer to their copies of the reader if they wish. Their questions may be on the context surrounding the passage, or on the passage itself.

- The groups then exchange the lists of questions, and the passages.

- Each group reads the new passage and then tries to answer the questions that they have been given.

It's on the Tip of my Tongue

Expand your students' vocabulary by building on their knowledge of the characters they have been reading about

Level	Elementary onwards
Activity type	Groupwork
Equipment/ Materials	Photocopies
Plus ...	A class set of activators, for example *The Longman Essential Activator, Oxford Wordpower*

- Looking back over what you have read so far, choose a paragraph from the class reader which describes one of the main characters in some detail.

- Type it out, changing all the specific language into more general terms, for example 'he strode purposefully into the room' becomes 'he walked purposefully into the room'. You may wish to underline the words that you have changed.

- Make one copy of your 'simplified' text for each pair of students.

- Put the class into small groups, and give each group a copy of the text. Using both their knowledge of the book, and the information provided by the context, they work to 'unsimplify' the text.

- Finally, the students compare their new texts with the original.

Missing Character

A character's gone missing – will your students' mini-portraits help the police to find him or her?

Level	Beginner to Pre-intermediate
Activity type	Pairwork/groupwork (optional)
Equipment/ Materials	OHP (optional)
Plus ...	A set of class readers and a 'missing person' poster (see below)

- Produce a typical 'missing person' poster for one of the characters in the class reader. Blank out his or her name and photocopy it onto an OHT if possible.

- Present the poster to your class. Ask them to say who it must be and why. Examine the language used in the poster.

- Put the students into pairs or small groups. Ask them to produce a 'missing person' poster for one character in the novel, but not to write the character's name on it.

- Display the posters round the classroom. The students have to guess who they refer to.

Lonely Hearts

Everybody needs somebody – even characters in a novel

Level	Pre-intermediate onwards
Activity type	Pairwork
Equipment/ Materials	Photocopies
Plus ...	A 'lonely hearts' column

- Make a copy of a lonely hearts column, one for each student. It can be very helpful to produce a glossary of common terms used in these columns, for example 'GSH' means 'good sense of humour.'

- Look at these together in class, discussing the language used.

- Tell your students that some of the characters in their reader are feeling lonely. Working in pairs, they should write a lonely hearts advertisement on behalf of one or two of them.

- Display these around the classroom.

Fantasy Casting

Arnold Schwarzenegger as Mr Darcy?

Level	Pre-intermediate onwards
Activity type	Groupwork
Equipment/ Materials	Photocopies
Plus ...	A cast list (see below)

- Produce a list of the characters in the book in the form of a cast list. Photocopy one for each group of students.

- Divide the class into small groups. Tell the students that they are casting directors working on the new Hollywood version of the class reader. They have to agree on a cast list for all the characters in the book. They have an unlimited budget – and may even choose actors who are no longer with us.

- Encourage disagreement.

Movie Screenplay

Bring the text to life/celluloid?

Level	Pre-intermediate onwards
Activity type	Groupwork
Equipment/ Materials	Photocopies

- Find three or four passages in the book with dramatic possibilities. These may be key scenes, involving several of the main characters. Photocopy each passage for the number of students in each group (see below).

- Divide the class into three or four groups. You may wish to vary the size of the groups depending on the number of characters in each scene.

- Give each group one of the passages. Ask them to read it, and to discuss what has happened up to that point in the story.

- The students then work in their groups to produce a screenplay for their scene, imagining that they are filming this episode. They draw up a list of characters, invent dialogue and could even discuss possible sound effects.

- When they have worked together on their screenplays, they cast the different character roles within their own group. They then rehearse the scene for a short time.

- Finally each group performs their scene for the rest of the class.

Instant Screenplay

From text to stage

Level	Pre-intermediate onwards
Activity type	Groupwork (optional)
Equipment/ Materials	None

- Choose a passage from the book which involves a number of characters, and is written using a lot of direct speech. It should be a passage with dramatic potential.

- Look at the passage as a class, discussing any issues of vocabulary and pronunciation, as well as talking about its context in the book.

- Allocate each of the speaking parts to a different student. Give another student the role of narrator. Ask them to read the passage aloud as if they were actors doing a 'read-through.' The narrator reads out all the parts that are not in direct speech.

- Now ask the students to read through the passage for a second time, this time trying to act it out as much as possible. They may use any furniture as props.

- Finally, ask them to put their books aside, and to re-enact the scene without the narrator, as they think it really happened.

- If you have a large class, put the students into smaller groups after the first read-through.

Reviews

Students help each other to choose readers

Level	Intermediate onwards
Activity type	Homework (optional)
Equipment/ Materials	Photocopies
Plus ...	One or two book reviews

- Look at one or two book reviews in class, discussing any issues of style and language.

- Ask each student to produce a review of the book that he or she is reading for the other students in the class.

- These reviews are then made available for everybody to read. They may be displayed in the classroom or in the school library, or they may be put into a reviews file so that any student can consult them.

Review Forms

Your students can be a resource too!

Level	Elementary to Intermediate
Activity type	Homework (optional)
Equipment/ Materials	Photocopies
Plus ...	A review form (see below)

- Either, produce a standard-style review form for your students.

- Or, ask your students what information would help them decide whether they would like to read a book or not. Working together they produce a form that, when filled in by a reader, would include this information.

- Photocopy the form and place the forms in the library and classroom. Whenever a student finishes a book, one of these forms should be completed.

- These reviews can then be made available for everybody to read.

Book Presentations

Make recent reading the basis for class talks

Level	Elementary onwards
Activity type	Whole class
Equipment/ Materials	None

- Tell the students about a novel that you have read recently. Describe the characters and elements of the plot. Try to give them an authentic flavour of the book. You may even choose to read passages from it. Make it interesting, but don't give away the ending.

- Organise a weekly slot for book presentations and encourage the students to sign up each week.

- Make it clear that their presentations can take different forms. They could be similar to the one that you have given. Alternatively, they could be question and answer sessions or student readings from the book.

Our Next Reader

Find out what everybody has been reading – and see what you are going to read next

Level	Elementary onwards
Activity type	Groupwork
Equipment/ Materials	None

- This activity works best when everybody in the class has been reading a different book.

- Put the students into groups of three or four, and ask them to take it in turns to tell the other students in the group about the book that they have been reading. Tell them to give some indication of the story, but not to give too much away. They take notes, and may wish to ask each other questions.

- When all the groups have presented all the readers, change the groupings, so that now everybody is next to someone they have not been sitting with before.

- Each person tells the other people in the group about the books that they have just heard about. They may wish to refer to their notes.

- When the group has heard about all the books that they have not read, they decide, as a group, which book they would most like to read next.

Story Soap Update

The great thing about soaps is that they just go on and on

Level	Elementary onwards
Activity type	Groupwork
Equipment/ Materials	None

- Make sure that you are reading a good book.

- On Monday, tell your students about it.

- On Wednesday, give them an update.

- On Thursday, or Friday, tell them what's happened now.

- Ask them what they are reading at the moment. Put them into 'reading groups' and tell them to fill in their classmates on the story so far.

- The following week, ask them to go into the same reading groups. They tell each other what has happened in their readers, since they last met. You may wish to make this a regular session.

Movie Moguls

Which graded readers are going to get the Hollywood treatment?

Level	Pre-intermediate onwards
Activity type	Mingle/open space activity
Equipment/ Materials	None

- This activity is particularly useful because it works even when some students in the class are reluctant to read in their own time. Give these students the role of 'movie moguls'.

- Tell your class that a number of Hollywood financiers are looking to English language graded class readers to provide their next blockbuster. Allocate the roles of these movie moguls to the less enthusiastic readers. The other students are 'ideas people' who are selling their latest idea – the book they have just been reading.

- Give each of the movie moguls a desk or 'office'. The ideas people should move round the classroom and visit each mogul in turn, explaining why their book will produce the next Hollywood blockbuster.

- At the end of the activity, the moguls explain which books they have chosen, giving their reasons.

5

Icebreakers and Welcoming Activities

The word 'icebreaker' has been part of English teaching terminology for a long time, which is probably a fair indication of the necessity for activities which can be used at the beginning of a course.

For adults, going into a classroom, a place capable of stimulating some possibly unpleasant memories, is hard enough, without the expectation that one will have to communicate to strangers, **and** in a foreign language.

For schoolchildren, the playful nature of language learning needs to be communicated when a group and a teacher are first brought together, if there is to be a positive working relationship.

Many private language schools bring students from a variety of cultures and backgrounds together, students who may have little in common, apart from a desire to learn English. It is necessary to 'start out on the right foot' if a group is to work purposefully together. The activities in this section aim to get students working together in English, with tasks that are challenging but not threatening. Many of them help students to get to know each other, to get used to one another's English, and to relax in an uncritical atmosphere.

Some activities also allow the teacher to stand back, observe group dynamics, and assess student needs. These activities may be used when a new group comes together, or when a teacher takes over an existing group. Some may be used in a school which operates a rolling intake, where new students need to be welcomed into a class which has already assumed an identity.

Person/Place/Object

A get-to-know-you activity that bypasses the more commonly discussed personal details

Level	Elementary onwards
Activity type	Mingle/open space activity
Equipment/ Materials	Labels

- Write on the board the names of a person, a place and an object that are important to you personally.

- Tell the students that they have to find out why the names on the board are important to you. You can only say 'yes' or 'no'. Guide them towards the correct answers, using fuller answers only if necessary.

- Once they have discovered the answers, tell each student to write on a label the names of a person, place or object that are important to them. Tell them that the three things should not be connected, for example not 'my boyfriend, his bike, and the place where we meet'.

- The students mingle, finding out as much information about one another as possible.

Ball Game 1

A lively way of learning each other's names and practising the language of introductions

Level	Beginner to Pre-intermediate
Activity type	Whole class
Equipment/ Materials	A ball

- Warm up the students by playing 'catch' briefly in the classroom.

- When the ball comes back to you say, 'This is Yoko [name of the student who threw the ball to you] and I'm Mark.'

- Throw the ball on to another student and, using gestures, make it clear that this person is now to introduce Yoko, yourself and him/herself to the class: 'This is Yoko, and this is Mark, and I'm Filipe.'

- This person then throws the ball to another member of the group who introduces those in the chain before them, before introducing themselves and throwing the ball on.

- This pattern continues until everyone has been introduced.

Ball Game 2

Add a bit of personal information and structural practice

Level	Pre-intermediate onwards
Activity type	Whole class
Equipment/ Materials	A ball

- Warm up the students by playing 'catch' briefly in the classroom.

- When the ball comes back to you, say, 'I'm Mark and I like playing football.'

- Throw the ball on to another student and, using gestures, make it clear that this person is now to introduce yourself and him/herself to the class, using a similar phrase for example, 'This is Mark, he likes watching football and I'm Filipe and I enjoy going to the opera.'

- This person then throws the ball to another member of the group who introduces those in the chain before them, before introducing themselves and throwing the ball on.

- This pattern continues until everyone has been introduced.

Famous Person Labels

Perfect practice for yes/no questions

Level	Elementary to Intermediate
Activity type	Mingle/open space activity
Equipment/ Materials	Labels

- Draw up a list of famous people whose names will be familiar to your students. Write one of these names on a sticky label for each student in the class.

- Ask the students to stand with their backs to you and place one label on each back. Allow the students to turn, mingle and examine each other's labels. Explain that the aim of the activity is to discover their new identity using only yes/no questions, for example, 'Am I a film star?'

- As homework, the students write a brief biography/description of the famous person that they have been allocated.

Pair Introductions 1

A more detailed introduction

Level	Beginner to Pre-intermediate
Activity type	Pairwork; homework
Equipment/ Materials	None

- Encourage the class to ask you simple questions, for example, 'Where were you born?' Write each question on the board and answer it. Continue until you have a list of about six questions. The number will depend on the level of the class.

- Working in pairs, the students ask each other the same questions. They may take notes if they want to.

- The students take it in turns to introduce their partner to the class, along with the information they have found out.

- For homework, the students use their notes to write a brief portrait of their partner. These portraits can be put up on the wall.

Pair Introductions 2

Encourage students to reflect on their own experience of learning

Level	Pre-intermediate onwards
Activity type	Pairwork
Equipment/ Materials	None

- Ask students to work in pairs and interview their partner about their previous experience of learning.

- Use this to lead into a group discussion on ways in which we learn a language. You may wish to use this discussion to help you when you are deciding on an appropriate syllabus for your students.

Families

An enjoyable activity that works particularly well with large classes and encourages question practice

Level	Elementary to Intermediate
Activity type	Mingle/open space activity
Equipment/ Materials	Slips of paper

- Give each student a slip of paper. Ask them to write three complete sentences about their family. Fewer sentences may work well with lower level classes.

- Collect the slips of paper and redistribute them randomly. Ask each student to think of the questions to find the person whose piece of paper they are holding. Help at this stage if necessary.

- The students then mingle to 'find' and 'be found'.

- Other useful topics include: houses, animals, hobbies, holidays.

This activity is an adaptation of an activity in *Classroom Dynamics* (Jill Hadfield, OUP).

World Map

(multinational classes only)
A lively activity that emphasises the students' varied backgrounds

Level	Elementary onwards
Activity type	Pairwork
Equipment/ Materials	None
Plus ...	A piece of coloured card (see below) and a wall map of the world

- Put the names of all the students into a 'hat'. Draw them out in pairs and seat the pairs together.

- The pairs interview each other about where they come from and students take notes.

- Each student then tells the class about their new friend.

- As homework, give each student a piece of coloured card. They should describe the place where their partner comes from (for example, 'Yun-Taek comes from Seoul, the capital of South Korea …').

- The next day each student is responsible for placing their card in the right place on a world map, using ribbons or pieces of string to show the exact location.

Pairing Games

Children enjoy this one and it's useful for breaking the ice in a class where students may already know each other, but are together as a group for the first time

Level	Beginner to Pre-intermediate
Activity type	Pairwork/mingle
Equipment/ Materials	Prepared cards

- Prepare cards with the name of one half of a famous couple or pair on each one for example, Mickey Mouse and Minnie Mouse.

- Hand the cards out to the students. Make sure that they can remember their new names and then ask them to find their partners. Encourage them to use simple language if possible, for example, 'Who are you?' 'Are you …?'

- When all the pairs are together, they can introduce themselves to the class adding additional information if they can, for example, 'Hi, I'm Minnie Mouse. I'm Mickey's girlfriend.'

Lying Game

Cynical teenagers, who might not be curious about one another, are happy to score points!

Level	Elementary onwards
Activity type	Competitive activity/game
Equipment/ Materials	None

- Tell the students three pieces of information about yourself, only one of which is true. The students may ask you any questions they wish to. Be prepared!

- The students discuss, in groups, which story they believe and, when everyone is ready, they deliver their verdict, giving their reasons. If you wish, points can be recorded on the board.

- The students then write three pieces of information about themselves. Again, only one is true.

- The game can then be repeated as above.

Conversation Dice

A good activity for lower-level students who may lack the confidence for free interaction

Level	Elementary onwards
Activity type	Whole class
Equipment/ Materials	A set of dice

- Prepare a list of tasks corresponding to the numbers on the dice, for example:

    4 = Tell the group about your family

    5 = Ask someone about their hobbies

- The students take it in turns to throw the dice. Each time they throw, they have to perform the task on the list that you have prepared. If a student throws the same number twice, he or she can either throw the dice again, or give more information.

- After ten minutes, when conversation is flowing freely, dispense with the dice.

Famous Couples

Sometimes it's easier to be relaxed when you're someone else

Level	Pre-intermediate onwards
Activity type	Pairwork/mingle
Equipment/ Materials	Labels

- Before the lesson, draw up a list of famous couples, for example, Antony and Cleopatra, Catherine Zeta Jones and Michael Douglas. Write each name on to a sticky label.

- As each student walks into the classroom, present them with a sticky label. The students mingle and try to find their partners. Once a couple is 'reunited' they sit together and brainstorm whatever they know about the couple that they have been allocated.

- When all the couples are seated, they take it in turns to present as much information as they can about their new identities. Encourage the other students to contribute.

- Now that the ice has been broken, the students may wish to discover more about one another's true identities.

6

Dialogues

Scripted dialogues have always been a part of language teaching, whether contrived and wooden, or authentic and fresh. They can be found in coursebooks, may be written by teachers themselves, or can be taken from radio, films or TV programmes.

In this section we are concerned with the use of short recorded dialogues and their transcripts, not primarily for developing listening skills, but as the basis for more intensive language work. Dialogues can be used to teach new vocabulary in a clear context, to present functional language, and to introduce new structures; as well as to present and practise stress, rhythm and intonation.

Before using a dialogue, it's always best to make sure that you are fully aware of the phonological features it contains. Marking the transcript for pronunciation, in the way that has been shown opposite (*Example Dialogues*), helps to remind you of these features – in addition to the target language. It can also serve as the basis for the students' written record.

In this section the activities are divided into two parts: *Presentations* and *Practice Activities*. These are cross-referenced so that it is clear which activities may most easily be combined within a single lesson.

Example Dialogues

1 Nightclub

Vic: Oh no! Not this track again!

Bob: I know. This is the third time he's played it tonight.

Vic: I wish he'd play something decent.

Bob: I know. This music's driving me up the wall.

2 Under the weather

Sue: Hi. How's things?

Jan: Fine. And you?

Sue: Well, I feel a bit under the weather, to be honest.

Jan: What's the matter?

Sue: I've got a terrible headache.

Jan: Have you tried taking an aspirin?

Sue: I have, but it didn't help.

Jan: Perhaps you should see a doctor.

Sue: I think I will.

Key
wavy line – intonation
black dot – secondary stress
white circle – primary stress

# Stressed Words	# Student Scribe	# Line-by-Line Prediction

Construct dialogues from stressed words

Listen and dictate

Listen and predict what is coming next

Level	Elementary onwards
Activity type	Pairwork/groupwork (optional)
Equipment/ Materials	Single cassette player; photocopies
Plus ...	A dialogue (see below)

may be followed by **Disappearing Dialogue, First-line Change, Parallel Situations**

- Find a short dialogue (of four to eight lines) which is appropriate for the level of your students. Listen to the dialogue and mark the stressed words on the transcript.

- Write these stressed words onto a set of cards or slips of paper, one set for each group of students.

- Play the recording of the dialogue to the students. Elicit the context in which the conversation took place and ask some comprehension questions.

- Put the class into groups and give each group one of the sets of the cards you have prepared. Explain that you are going to play the dialogue again.

- In their groups, the students have to arrange the stressed words in the order in which they hear them. Play the recording twice if necessary.

- Ask the groups to reconstruct the dialogue as best they can, using the stressed words on the cards. When they have finished this, write an agreed version of the dialogue on the board.

- Listen again and correct the version on the board focusing on the target language, before marking phonological features.

Level	All levels
Activity type	Whole class
Equipment/ Materials	Single cassette player
Plus ...	A dialogue (see below)

may be followed by **Disappearing Dialogue, First-line Change, Parallel Situations**

- Choose a dialogue (of four to eight lines) that you feel will be challenging for your students. They may understand the gist, but will only be able to decipher it completely after listening to the dialogue a number of times.

- Give one student in the class the cassette-recorder. Make sure that the tape is in the right place.

- Ask another student to stand at the board and give him or her a board pen. This person is the class 'scribe' and is not allowed to speak.

- Explain to the class that they are going to hear a dialogue. Their aim is to tell the class scribe what to write on the board, in order to produce an exact transcript. They can ask the student with the cassette-recorder to pause and replay parts of the dialogue as many times as they like. Remind them of the language they will need in order to do this.

- When the class has completed this task to your satisfaction, focus on the target language before marking the transcript for phonological features and drilling.

Level	Elementary onwards
Activity type	Whole class
Equipment/ Materials	Single cassette player; OHP (optional)
Plus ...	A dialogue (see below)

may be followed by any practice activity

- This activity works best with dialogues of four to six lines. It is ideal for presenting new language.

- Set the scene for the dialogue through a discussion, or use pictures or realia.

- Play the first line of the dialogue. Ask comprehension questions and build up the context in greater detail.

- Play the line again and get the students to repeat it accurately both in terms of language and pronunciation.

- Ask the students to predict the next line. Discuss their predictions and then play the second line. Deal with any comprehension problems. Then drill the first two lines, first in closed pairs and then in open pairs.

- Ask the students to predict the next line. Continue in this way, until the whole dialogue has been practised.

- Write the dialogue on the board with the students' help or project it using a photocopied OHT.

- Focus on the target language, and discuss stress, intonation and other phonological features, marking the transcript where necessary.

Split-completion Dialogue

Create a dialogue and work on discourse features

Level	Pre-intermediate onwards
Activity type	Pairwork
Equipment/ Materials	OHP (optional); photocopies
Plus ...	A dialogue (Example Dialogue 2, page 36)

may be followed by **First-line Change, Parallel Situations**

- You will need: copies of the dialogue for half the class, with Sue's lines deleted; copies of the dialogue for the other half of the class, with Jan's lines deleted; and a copy of the dialogue for each student in the class with Sue and Jan's lines deleted, leaving only their names followed by a dotted line.

- Put the students into pairs. Give one student in each pair Sue's lines, and the other, Jan's lines. Tell them to look carefully at their parts of the dialogue and to work individually to try to fill in the missing lines.

- When they have completed this, give all the students a copy of the 'names only' dialogue. Individually, they should transfer the new lines that they have written onto this sheet of paper. Take back the original sheets at this point.

- In pairs, the students read their lines, producing a somewhat disjointed dialogue. Each pair then works to repair their own dialogue so that it reads more coherently.

- The students perform their dialogues.

- Look at the original dialogues. Discuss the differences.

Cut-up Dialogue

Rearrange lines to form a cohesive dialogue

Level	All levels
Activity type	Pairwork
Equipment/ Materials	Photocopies
Plus ...	A dialogue (see below)

may be followed by **Ray's Method, First-line Change, Parallel Situations**

- Choose a dialogue of about four to eight lines. Make a photocopy of the dialogue for each pair in the class. Cut up each photocopy line by line and put these lines into an envelope.

- Give one of these envelopes to each pair of students. Ask them to put the lines into the correct order.

- Play the dialogue. The students listen to check.

- Show the students a copy of the original dialogue, using either the board, a photocopied OHT, or photocopies.

- Focus on the target language, and discuss stress, intonation and other phonological features, marking the transcript where necessary.

Disappearing Dialogue

Learn a dialogue as it is gradually being erased

Level	All levels
Activity type	Pairwork
Equipment/ Materials	None
Plus ...	A dialogue (see below)

may follow **Stressed Words, Student Scribe, Line-by-Line Prediction**

- Choose a dialogue of about four to eight lines. Begin the activity with the whole dialogue written clearly on the board.

- Put the students into pairs. Ask them to act out the dialogue, reading from the board.

- When they have done this, ask one of the students to erase the stressed words from the board. This may involve a degree of negotiation between the students, if the stressed words have not already been marked.

- In pairs, the students act out the dialogue again.

- Ask another student to erase words in another category, for example the verb forms.

- Once again, the students act out the rapidly-disappearing dialogue. This process may be continued until the board is almost, or completely blank.

- Provide the students with a written record of the dialogue.

First-line Change

Adapt a dialogue to follow a new first line

Level	All levels
Activity type	Pairwork/mingle
Equipment/ Materials	Slips of paper
Plus ...	A dialogue (see below)

may follow any presentation and controlled practice

- On slips of paper, write a number of different lines which might start dialogues similar, or parallel to Example Dialogue 1. Alternatives to 'Oh no! Not this track again' might be 'Oh no! Not this episode again.' 'Oh no! Not this commercial again.' 'Oh no! Not this dialogue presentation again.'

- Give these slips of paper to half the students in your class. Ask the students to mingle. When a person with a slip meets a person without one, they start a conversation using their line and develop it along similar lines to the previously practised dialogue.

Ray's Method

Help one another to learn a dialogue

Level	All levels
Activity type	Pairwork/mingle
Equipment/ Materials	Photocopies
Plus ...	A dialogue (Example Dialogue 2, page 36)

may follow **Stressed Words**, **Line-by-Line Prediction**, **Cut-up Dialogue**

- In order to use this activity, you need the following: copies of the dialogue for half the class, with some of the words in Sue's lines gapped; and copies of the dialogue for the other half of the class, with some of the words in Jan's lines gapped.

- Put the students into pairs, give them the copies of the dialogue and ask them to act it out. If the student who is acting out Sue is unable to remember the missing words, 'Jan' should help her. If the student who is acting out Jan is unable to remember her missing words, 'Sue' should help her.

- Once they have done this, the class mingle. Any 'Sue' may find any 'Jan' and act out the dialogue with her.

- When this has gone on for a while, the students exchange roles and transcripts and continue in their new roles.

- Finally, the students return to their original pairs and act out the dialogue.

- Provide the students with a written record of the dialogue. In this case, they may fill in their gapped version.

Parallel Situations

Adapt what has been learnt to a new situation

Level	Elementary onwards
Activity type	Pairwork/groupwork/ mingle
Equipment/ Materials	None
Plus ...	A dialogue (Example Dialogue 1, page 36)

may follow any presentation and controlled practice

- Ask the students to stand in an open space. Ask them to find a partner and act out Example Dialogue 1 as best they can.

- The students mingle and then find another partner to act out another similar dialogue.

- Tell them that something has changed. You may wish to change the roles they are in. For example, Sue is now a doctor and Jan a patient; or you may wish to change the situation, for example, Sue now has hayfever.

7

Warmers and Fillers

Everybody needs warmers and fillers. Warmers come at the beginning of a lesson; fillers in the middle or at the end. When an activity is used as a warmer, the teacher's aim may be to get the students talking and thinking in English, motivating them and getting them to think about the topic to come. The aim may also be to get the students working as a group. Or again it may be to avoid a predictable beginning to each lesson, for example, 'Turn to page 113.'

When an activity is used as a filler, the teacher's aim may be to provide a change of pace, fill an awkward gap or finish off the lesson on a positive and purposeful note. On a linguistic level, warmers and fillers can be used to recycle previously taught language, as well as diagnose problems before an input stage or test after new language has been introduced. They can be used to practise the four skills of speaking, listening, reading and writing.

It's worth trying a range of activities with your students, so that you find which ones work best. These can then become regular sessions, giving your students something to look forward to, and providing continuity within the class syllabus.

Make a Paper Aeroplane

Giving instructions in a foreign language can be hard ... and the results hilarious!

Level	Elementary onwards
Activity type	Pairwork/groupwork (optional)
Equipment/ Materials	Scrap paper

- Ask the students whether they know how to make a paper aeroplane.

- Divide the class into pairs or small groups, but group them so that there is at least one student who knows how to in each group. At lower levels, pre-teach any essential vocabulary.

- Ask the 'experts' to explain to their partner(s) how to make and fly a paper aeroplane. Their partner(s) is given a piece of paper and is either blindfolded, or asked to keep his/her eyes shut.

- At lower levels, ask the students to write the instructions. At higher levels, encourage the students to think of the activity as a roleplay. The 'expert' is sighted and is telling a blind friend how to make a plane, and then has to describe how it flies and where it lands.

- Other tasks that work with this activity are origami (Japanese paper-folding), making the perfect cup of tea or coffee, and starting a car.

One-Word Story on Paper

An invaluable activity to practise basic writing skills at all levels

Level	All levels
Activity type	Whole class
Equipment/ Materials	Scrap paper

- This activity works best when the students are seated in a circle, or horseshoe, with desks in front of them.

- Explain to the students that they are going to tell a story, but that they are only allowed to contribute one word at a time. Begin the story yourself with the word *the*.

- Ask the first student to continue the story with the next word. Each student then continues the story by adding one word. At lower levels write the story on the board as it progresses. Correct any mistakes as they occur by using gesture. In a monolingual class, this activity can be demonstrated by using the students' native language.

- Give each student a sheet of paper. Ask them to write the first word of a story. They then pass the piece of paper to the left and write one word to continue the story on the piece of paper that they have been handed.

- Repeat this. If a student receives a story and feels that the last word is impossible, they pass it back for correction. You may have to adjudicate.

- Finally students read out the stories.

First Letter, Last Letter

A pronunciation game that's really a spelling game

Level	Elementary to Intermediate
Activity type	Mingle/competitive activity
Equipment/ Materials	None

- Ask the students to stand in a circle. Tell one student to say any word at all.

- Tell the student to his or her left to say a word that begins with the last letter of the previous word, the next student continues in the same manner, for example, '**p**ea**ch** ... **h**ous**e** ... **e**nginee**r** ... .' When problems arise you should adjudicate.

- To make the activity into a game, give students a five-second limit to each word. If they do not say an appropriate word in the time allowed, they have to leave the circle.

Spelling Game

Your students will enjoy playing this at breaktime too!

Level	Pre-intermediate onwards
Activity type	Pairwork/competitive activity
Equipment/ Materials	None

- Divide the class into teams. Each team takes it in turns to add a letter to a word. Each letter must contribute to a word in English, but the team which *completes* a word loses and the opposing team is awarded a point.

- For example:

  Team A says 'A.' Team B says 'N.' *Team B loses and Team A wins one point.*

  Team B says 'C.' Team A says 'A.' Team B says 'R.' *Team B loses and Team A wins one point.*

- If a team feels that the opposing team has used a letter which does not build a word in English, they may challenge. If the opposing team is unable to produce a word, the team challenging gains one point. If a challenge is incorrect, the other team gains one point.

- For example:

  Team A says 'M'. Team B says 'Z'. *Team A challenges and wins a point.*

  Team B says 'A'. Team A says 'A'. *Team B challenges. Team A says 'Aardvark' and gains one point.*

- The best way to explain this game to your class is to demonstrate it.

Alphabet Race

Simple but effective and can be used for revision or as a warmer for a new vocabulary area

Level	Elementary onwards
Activity type	Competitive activity/game
Equipment/ Materials	None

- Put the students into pairs or small groups. Ask one student in each group to write the alphabet vertically down the side of a piece of paper (or you may wish to photocopy some sheets in advance).

- Write a topic on the board and give the students a time limit. They have to write one word related to that topic beginning with each letter of the alphabet on their sheet of paper. Check the spelling or tell the students to check it in dictionaries. The group with the most words wins.

- One way of extending the activity is to circulate the sheets round different groups. The students note down any new vocabulary and may challenge any inappropriate words or spelling mistakes. Expect heated debate.

The Rhinoceros Game

A livelier version of the previous activity – good with small classes, and very popular with children

Level	All levels
Activity type	Competitive activity/game
Equipment/ Materials	Different coloured board pens

- Put your students into two teams. Ask them to come up with a long word, for example *rhinoceros*. Write this word down the left side of the board and again down the centre, once for each team. Make sure that you have left enough space between them for each team to write a word across.

- Tell the students that each team has to write one word across for each letter of the long word. Limit the words to a particular group: at lower levels, for example, verbs, nouns etc; at higher levels, words connected with crime, cars etc.

  For example:

  Robber
  House-breaker
  Innocent
  N ...

- Give each team a different coloured board pen and ask them to go to the back of the classroom. One member of each team then runs to the front of the class to write a word. He or she runs back to hand the pen to another member of the team. The first team to complete all the words across wins.

Busybodies

*Students insist on sidetracking you?
Take advantage*

Level	Elementary onwards
Activity type	Pairwork
Equipment/ Materials	None

- Allocate each of the students a question word, for example 'Why?' 'Where?' 'Did?' Explain that you are going to tell them about your morning, starting from when you woke up. Their task is to stop you arriving at the school by asking you too many questions. Give them a time limit. Make it longer if the class is more advanced.

- Once you have demonstrated the activity, you can get the students to play it in pairs. But this time the students are not limited to one question word.

Thanks to Richard Side for this idea.

Just a Minute

*A variation on the well-known BBC
radio show*

Level	Intermediate onwards
Activity type	Competitive activity/game
Equipment/ Materials	A watch (a stopwatch is ideal); cards

- Write on cards some topics that your class will feel confident talking about, for example 'My house' 'My last holiday'. You may wish to use the cards for Summaries Circle (*Circles*).

- Ask a more confident student to take a card at random and read the topic aloud to the group. Explain that the aim of the game is for this student to talk on this subject for one minute without hesitating or making a serious grammatical error.

- Tell the other students to challenge if they feel that rules have been broken. You will need to adjudicate here. If the challenge is accepted, the challenger has to speak on the same subject for the remaining time. The student speaking at the end of the minute wins a point.

- Continue the game with another student and a new topic card.

Anything in the World

*Twenty Questions or Animal,
Vegetable or Mineral – classic practice
of forming questions*

Level	Elementary onwards
Activity type	Competitive activity/game
Equipment/ Materials	None

- Think of an object, animate or inanimate, anything in the world. Tell the students that they have to find out what you are thinking of by asking 'yes/no' questions. If you like, you can limit the number of questions, or have a time limit.

- The student who asks the final question, for example 'Is it an ant?' then thinks of the next 'thing'. The game continues.

Yes/No – Black/White Game

Good practice for all kinds of questions

Level	Elementary onwards
Activity type	Competitive activity/game
Equipment/ Materials	None

- Ask one student to sit in the 'hot seat'. Tell this person that his or her aim is to survive for one minute without saying 'yes,' 'no,' 'black,' or 'white'. Tell the other students that it is their aim to force the person in the hot seat to use one of these words.

- For example:

    'Do you live in Paris?'
    'You know that I do.'

    'Have you been to Switzerland?'
    'Never.'

    'You just said "no," didn't you?'
    'No, I didn't… agh!!'

Class Expert

Give your students valuable question practice with this activity

Level	Intermediate onwards
Activity type	Whole class
Equipment/ Materials	None

- Ask the class to think about subjects or topic areas which they, as individuals, know a lot about, for example: English football, banking, their own country (in a multilingual class).

- Make a list of the students' names and put it up on a noticeboard in the classroom. Ask each student to write their topic next to their name. Explain that, over the coming weeks, you would like the students to take it in turns to answer questions on their chosen area.

- When all the students have written up a topic, find a student who is willing to start the ball rolling. Introduce both the student and his or her topic area to the class, and invite the other students to ask questions or simply to check the things they *think* they know about the 'expert's' chosen area, for example 'Are there many Italian players in English teams?' 'There are four leagues in English football, aren't there?'

- If you wish to extend the activity, ask the students to write down, on a piece of paper, anything new that they have learnt during the session. They should hand these slips to the 'expert' for checking.

Absent Friends

A warmer to use when your class arrives in dribs and drabs – it may even encourage them to arrive on time!

Level	Pre-intermediate onwards
Activity type	Whole class
Equipment/ Materials	None

- Ask the class to imagine where their absent classmates are, and what they might be doing. Take each student in turn and record the class's guesses. When the student arrives, they can tell the class whether they were right or not.

- Excellent practice for modal verbs and adverbs. For example 'He can't have missed his bus again. He's probably just stuck in traffic.'

In My Grandmother's Chest

A children's favourite which emphasises the adjective-noun word order in English

Level	Elementary and Pre-intermediate
Activity type	Competitive activity/game
Equipment/ Materials	None

- *Teacher:* 'In my grandmother's chest, I found an angry ant.'

  Student 1: 'In my grandmother's chest, I found an angry ant and a big book.'

  Student 2: 'In my grandmother's chest, I found an angry ant, a big book and a clever cat.'

- Encourage the class to continue as above. Stop at Z.

Stress

Practise stress by getting rid of it.

Level	Beginner to Intermediate
Activity type	Competitive activity/game
Equipment/ Materials	Large sheets of paper and drawing pins
Plus ...	Teacher's knowledge of phonemic chart

- Make a list of at least twenty recently-taught words which conform to four different stress patterns, for example 'Tuesday… Saturday… December… July.' Make four posters with the four stress patterns clearly marked, for example '**Oo… Ooo… oOo… oO.**' Place these posters around the room.

- Ask your students to go into the middle of the room. Tell them to run to the appropriate poster for the word which you read out.

- Work through the list of words in this way. If there is any disagreement, repeat the word until everybody is in the same place. When there is total agreement, everybody shouts out the word together.

- This activity also works well with individual phonemes. Used regularly it can be an effective way of teaching, and learning, the phonemic chart, especially for children.

Stupid Instructions

A different angle on giving instructions and warnings

Level	Beginner to Pre-intermediate
Activity type	Groupwork
Equipment/ Materials	Labels

- Explain to your students that some companies are now so scared of being sued that in England you can buy a packet of peanuts that carries the following warning: 'Contains nuts.' An American airline gives the following message: 'Instructions: Open packet, eat contents.'

- Divide your class into groups. Give each group a generous number of labels and a different coloured pen. Their task is to write as many 'stupid instructions' or warnings for objects in the classroom, as they can in an allocated time.

- As soon as they have written an instruction, they label the object. At the end of the activity, the class decides on the funniest instructions.

Drawing Race

Prepositions, shapes and much more

Level	Elementary to Intermediate
Activity type	Groupwork/ competitive activity
Equipment/ Materials	None
Plus ...	Quick drawings that you have produced

- Produce a number of quick drawings with a board pen, made up of shapes, objects – whatever you want. These should be simple drawings that another person would find easy to reproduce.

- Put your class into two or three teams (depending on the numbers in your class). Instruct one member of each team, the 'drawers,' to stand in front of the whiteboard with a board pen. Allocate each team a section of the whiteboard and a different coloured board pen.

- Sitting in front of the whiteboard, show the first drawing to everybody in the class, except those at the board. Explain that the drawers have to reproduce the pictures, as accurately and as quickly as possible, on the whiteboard. The other members of the team are to instruct them. Enjoy the chaos!

- You may wish to deal with any language problems before proceeding to the next picture, using new students as drawers. When things get really noisy, ask your students to sit on their hands.

Taxi Ride

A quick warmer that makes students aware of a valuable language-learning aid: themselves

Level	All levels
Activity type	Pairwork
Equipment/ Materials	None

- Put the students into pairs. Ask them to sit side by side and imagine that they are in a taxi. The student on the right is an English taxi-driver.

- Tell the student on the left that their aim is to keep the conversation going for a given time.

- Repeat the activity from time to time, each time extending the duration of the activity.

Thanks to Madrid taxi drivers for this activity.

Phoneme Labels

Great with a large class

Level	Pre-intermediate onwards
Activity type	Mingle/open space activity
Equipment/ Materials	Labels
Plus ...	Teacher's knowledge of phoneme chart; one different phoneme written on each label

- Write the phonemic chart out on a set of labels (in other words, 47 labels). The labels that you choose each time that you do the activity will depend on the number of students in your class, and the sounds which you wish to practise.

- Ask the class to stand. Give each student a different phoneme to wear. Make sure that everyone knows which sound they are wearing.

- 'Conduct' the class: first, each student you point to has to utter their own sound; second, all the other students have to chorus the sound; finally, move two students together to combine their sounds to make a word in English. Do this a few times to prepare the students for the next stage.

- Tell the students to mingle, looking for other students with whom they can make a word. A word may have any number of syllables. When a group forms, they chorus the word. You should check their answers.

- At the end of the activity, ask the students, 'Who could form the most words?' The chances are that it will be the student who is wearing the 'schwa'.

8

Circles

Circle activities are a way of providing a structure which enables and encourages students to interact in small groups. They take students out from behind their desks and away from their textbooks.

The activities which follow share a format. They give a variety of structures or frameworks for student interaction (for example, round the circle, across the circle, within the circle, circles within circles, students outside and students inside the circle). These frameworks give less confident students a space within which they can practise their English, as well as giving more confident students a more defined role. They can also be used for classes with poor dynamics.

Circle activities can be used for the presentation, practice, testing and recycling of grammar, vocabulary and pronunciation, as well as for fluency practice and needs analysis. When a circle is used for presentation it will normally include the whole class. However, a large class may be divided into smaller circles for practice.

Circles require minimal preparation and are extremely flexible. They are excellent lessons to 'have up your sleeve' for occasions when you are asked to teach with little or no warning.

Students

Keiko

Inger   Peter

Joon   Juan

Fritz   Maria

Luka

Summaries Circle

Ideal for the beginning of a course to help you with needs analysis

Level	All levels
Activity type	Whole class
Equipment/ Materials	Prepared cards
Plus ...	Two clipboards and Summaries Circle cards

- Ask Keiko to take one of the topic cards, for example 'my last holiday' and to read it to the group. Tell the others that they can ask Keiko any questions about her last holiday. Give the clipboard to Luka and explain that his role is: firstly, to take notes during the conversation; and secondly, when all the questions have dried up, to give a summary of the topic discussed to the whole group.

- When Luka has given his summary, it is Peter's turn to take a card and Fritz's turn to act as note-taker. This process then continues around the group. The note-takers help to ensure that any misunderstandings are cleared up.

- You may need to 'feed in' some language if the note-taker has any problems asking for repetition or clarification. Take notes on other problem areas and follow the activity with a mistakes session.

Example Cards

> **my last holiday**

> **my home**

Auxiliary Verb Circle

Learners are often surprised to discover the way the auxiliary verb moves like a beachball between English speakers

Level	Beginner to Pre-intermediate
Activity type	Pairwork (optional)
Equipment/ Materials	Prepared cards
Plus ...	Auxiliary Verb Circle cards

- **Forming questions** Give the cards to Keiko. She reads the card on the top of the pack to Luka, who turns the sentence into a yes/no question. Keiko then passes the cards to Peter, who reads the next sentence to Fritz. Go once round the circle in this way.

- **Answering questions** Go round the group again. This time Keiko looks at the card and transforms the sentences herself into a yes/no question for Luka, for example, 'Have you got a car?' Luka answers this in any way he likes. You may however wish to 'feed in' the standard auxiliary verb reply i.e. 'No, I haven't'.

- **Agreeing** Using one of the cards model 'Nor have I' and 'So have I'. The easiest way to do this is to join the circle yourself. Use the activity to practise these responses, for example 'Have you got a car?' 'Yes, I have' 'So have I'.

- **Differing** In the same way, model other responses such as 'Have you?' and 'I haven't' and then use the activity to practise them.

- Repeat the activity once more, telling the students they can now respond in any way they like, and encourage them to keep the conversation going for as long as possible. With a large class, this works best if the circle is split into pairs.

- Give each pair a card, which they can use to initiate conversation. When they have finished, they should pass the card on around the circle. In this way all the students will be involved in simultaneous free practice.

Example Cards

> **I'm in my 20s.**

> **I've got a car.**

A full set of Example Cards can be found on page 90.

Reporting Circle (Lower)

An activity which presents and practises the basic reporting verbs **said**, **told** *and* **asked**

Level	Elementary to Intermediate
Activity type	Groupwork (optional)
Equipment/ Materials	Slips of paper; prepared cards
Plus ...	Reporting Circle (Lower) cards

- Give the cards to Keiko and ask her to read the top card to Luka. Luka then has to report back the sentence that has been written on it, for example: 'I like ice-cream', 'She told me she liked ice-cream' or 'She said she liked ice-cream'.

- If Luka has problems, encourage the other students to help with the reporting verb or structure. Put the agreed verbs on the board along with the structure (see Key page 92). Discuss the change in the verb form and move on to the next pair (Peter and Fritz).

- Continue in this way until all the verbs and structures have been elicited. If you do the activity using the cards in the order suggested, the differences between the verbs, and the structures that they require, will be made clear to the students.

- Shuffle the cards and repeat the activity for further practice. With a large group you may wish to produce a greater number of cards for this stage of the activity.

- If the students are sufficiently confident, they may enjoy producing their own cards in small groups, for other groups to use.

Example Cards

1
I like ice cream.

2
I'm going to watch TV tonight.

Reporting Circle (Upper)

An activity which makes practising reporting verbs fun

Level	Intermediate onwards
Activity type	Whole class
Equipment/ Materials	Slips of paper; prepared cards
Plus ...	Reporting Circle (Upper) cards

- Give the cards to Keiko and ask her to read the top card to Luka. Luka has to report back the sentence that has been written on it, for example: 'Get out and don't come back!' – 'She told me to get out and not to come back'. If Luka has problems, encourage the other students to help with the reporting verb or structure.

- Put the agreed verb on the board and move to the next pair – Peter and Fritz. Continue in this way until all the verbs and structures have been elicited. If you do the activity using the cards in the order suggested, the verbs on the board can be grouped easily according to the structure that follows.

- Shuffle the cards and repeat the activity for further practice.

- Give the students three or four slips of paper each, telling them to choose verbs from the list on the board and to write on their slips phrases that correspond to the verbs, for example: 'Let's go to the beach' (*to suggest*). Allow them to use their course material or an appropriate reference book.

- Repeat the activity, using the slips they have produced. Keep the best examples to use for a later recycling activity.

Example Cards

1
Get out and don't come back!

2
If I were you, I'd take it back to the shop.

A full set of Example Cards can be found on pages 91-92.

Quickfire Circle

How to prepare for those idiomatic opening gambits that native speakers use so often!

Level	Pre-intermediate onwards
Activity type	Whole class
Equipment/ Materials	Prepared cards
Plus ...	Quickfire Circle cards

- Make up a set of cards. Those provided here are suitable for advanced students; you may wish to make your own, appropriate to the level of your students.

- Pass the cards out to all but one of the students. This student is in the 'hot seat'. Students take it in turns to read their lines, going round the circle. The person in the hot seat responds as best he or she can. At this stage welcome any peer support or correction.

- When all the cards have been read, repeat the procedure again with different students in the hot seat. You may need to repeat this stage four or five times before the whole group is familiar with the new expressions.

- When you feel the group is ready, put the cards on the floor in the middle of the circle. Invite two students sitting opposite each other to stand up. One of the students takes a card and reads it to the other, who responds. If they can, the pair continue the conversation.

- When the improvisation comes to an end, invite another pair to stand up and do the same.

Example Cards

What time do you call this?

Where to, guv?

Interview Circle

Intensive, noisy, free practice

Level	Elementary onwards
Activity type	Pairwork/groupwork
Equipment/ Materials	None
Plus ...	a job advertisement

- As a class, study the job advertisement. Discuss the kind of person who might get the job and make a list of the qualities and experience that this person might have.

- Explain that half the students are applicants for the post advertised, and that the other students are going to interview them. With a lower-level group, give them time to prepare before proceeding to the next stage.

- Ask the students to sit in two circles, one inside the other. Each circle must have the same number of seats (you may need to join in to make the numbers even). The chairs in the inner circle face out, and the chairs in the outer circle face in. The students in the inner circle are the applicants; and those in the outer circle, the interviewers. If you have more than fourteen students, make two sets of circles.

- Conduct all the interviews in pairs simultaneously. Give them a time limit.

- When the time has elapsed, ask the interviewers in the outer circle to move round one place to the left. They will now be facing a new applicant. They interview this applicant for the job.

- This process should continue until everybody in the inner circle has been interviewed by everybody in the outer circle.

- At the end, the interviewers meet to discuss who should get the job. The applicants discuss which interviewer they thought was most successful.

A full set of Example Cards can be found on page 94.

Waiting-room Circle

An amusing roleplay which helps students to practise both functional English and reporting

Level	Pre-intermediate onwards
Activity type	Groupwork
Equipment/ Materials	None
Plus ...	A set of cards with short/long lists of symptoms on them

- Explain to the students in the circle that they are in a waiting-room. They are waiting to consult a new doctor, about whom they are all very curious. You may wish to prepare the students either by giving each of them a list of their symptoms, or by allowing them to choose their own from a longer list. These should have been pre-taught.

- Ask one of the students to take the role of the doctor. Seat this person outside the circle. The patients take it in turns to visit the doctor, who asks them numerous questions about their symptoms and lifestyle, makes a diagnosis and gives advice. The patients return to the group and the doctor calls in the next patient from the circle.

- While the doctor is consulting his or her second patient, the first patient reports his or her consultation to the others in the waiting-room. This must be in as great a detail as possible, so that the full range of reporting verbs and language is used. Encourage the students to gossip.

- This activity can be used for other situations, such as visiting the bank manager and consulting a fortune-teller.

Make or *Do* Circle Game

An enjoyable revision activity for 'make' and 'do' that works well with children

Level	Elementary and Pre-intermediate
Activity type	Competitive activity/game
Equipment/ Materials	None

- Place your students in a standing circle. Begin the activity yourself by saying 'Every day I make my bed.' Accompany this with an appropriate mime.

- Ask the student next to you to repeat what you do, changing the case as appropriate, and using the mime, ask them to add another expression and associated mime. 'Every day my teacher makes his bed (*mime*), and I do my homework (*mime*).'

- The next student in the circle should repeat the previous statement and add his or her own. At this stage you should leave the circle. The activity will continue without you.

- If a student is unable to think of a new *make* or *do* expression, or forgets a previous expression or mime, they have to leave the circle. The last student remaining is the winner.

Collocation Circle

A proven way of learning by heart collocations previously presented in class

Level	Elementary onwards
Activity type	Whole class
Equipment/ Materials	None
Plus ...	A list of collocations, Idioms or phrasal verbs that you wish to teach

- Place your students in a circle. Elicit the first collocation on your list, for example 'deeply hurt'. Give the collocation an appropriate gesture. Whenever they see this gesture, they should chorus the collocation. Test them a couple of times.

- Elicit the next collocation on your list. Ask the person on your left to think of a gesture. Revise the two collocations by giving your own gesture, followed by the person on your left giving his or hers.

- The next student in the circle takes responsibility for providing a gesture for another of your collocations in the same way. Practise again, using the three gestures invented so far.

- When all the students have a collocation and a gesture, go round the circle. Each student elicits their own collocation by using their own gesture.

- Finally the students take it in turns to test each other by using a variety of gestures to elicit the collocations.

Thanks to Chris Campbell for this idea.

9

Questionnaires

Producing their own questionnaires can help students in a variety of ways. Firstly, it allows them the time to formulate questions before they use them in a communicative context.

Secondly, students gain in confidence when they are able to use language that they have produced themselves, and know to be correct. This then provides a solid foundation for more spontaneous interaction.

Questionnaires are particularly useful for recycling language, both within a semi-controlled framework, and subsequently in a freer context.

In native-speaking countries questionnaires can help students to prepare themselves for confident interaction with native speakers, as well as providing the context in which students may approach members of the public.

Question Types

Encourage your students to use a variety of question types in their questionnaires, for example:

- open-ended questions

- yes/no questions

- wh- questions

- true/false statements

- multiple choice

- ranking four items in order of importance, preference etc.

- 'finish the sentence' or gap-fill sentences

- 'what would you do if … ?' questions

In the Hot Seat

Prepare a questionnaire for an English-speaking guest

Level	Pre-intermediate onwards
Activity type	Groupwork; homework
Equipment/ Materials	Photocopies

- Tell the class that a 'guest' is coming into the classroom, and is willing to be interviewed in English.

- Put the students into groups and ask them to write down any questions that they would like to ask this person.

- Each group reads out their questions. Write these up on the board. Very often the groups will have produced similar questions; you can encourage the students to discuss which questions are most appropriate, and why.

- The students then decide the order in which their questions should be asked. A student or you yourself can take notes, writing down the questions in the suggested order.

- When a list of questions has been written down it should be photocopied. Give one copy to each student before the visitor is invited in.

- The students, in turn, ask each question on the questionnaire and take notes on the interviewee's answers. Warn students that the need for further questions might arise as a result of their guest's answers. They should feel free to ask these questions before another student moves onto the next scripted question.

Interview Questionnaire

From interview to article and back again

Level	Pre-intermediate onwards
Activity type	Pairwork
Equipment/ Materials	Photocopies
Plus ...	A newspaper article (see below)

- Choose carefully a newspaper article which takes the form of a character portrait of an interesting person. Photocopy one for each student in the class.

- Give it to the students to read.

- Ask the students, in pairs, to write the questions that the interviewer must have asked in order to find the information in the article, and to write these down in the form of a questionnaire.

- Review the questions as a class. The students may wish to add to the questionnaires that they have produced.

- Finally, the students roleplay the interview, working in their original pairs; one taking the part of the interviewer, the other the part of the interviewee.

Grammar Revision

Students ask and answer questions using a structure that you have allocated them

Level	Elementary to Intermediate
Activity type	Groupwork/mingle
Equipment/ Materials	None

- Before the lesson, decide on four or five structures that you wish to revise.

- Put the students into small groups. Allocate each student one of the structures that you wish to revise, for example the present perfect.

- Ask each student to write five questions that he or she could ask any other student within the class, for example: 'Have you been to Spain?' or 'Have you had breakfast this morning?'

- Ask the students to check the questions written by other members of their own group.

- The students then mingle with the rest of the class, and ask each other their questions. Tell the students that if they are asked what they think is an ungrammatical question, then they should call you.

- When all the questions have been asked, the students return to their groups and discuss what they have discovered.

Guess Who? Questionnaire

Guess who fell in love when she was nine

Level	Elementary onwards
Activity type	Pairwork/mingle
Equipment/ Materials	None

- Put the students into pairs. Ask them to discuss what they would most like to know about the other people in the class, and to produce two copies of a questionnaire in order to find out this information.

- The students mingle, asking questions, answering questions, and occasionally saying 'I'd rather not say' where necessary.

- As a class, the students take it in turns to give one piece of information that they have discovered. But they must not mention the name of the person concerned, for example 'Guess who's been to Disneyland.' The other class members have to guess who the sentence is about.

Reverse Questionnaire

Students inadvertently produce a questionnaire on the board

Level	Elementary and Pre-intermediate
Activity type	Pairwork; homework
Equipment/ Materials	None

- Divide the board into two columns. In the narrow, left-hand column write a piece of information about yourself, for example '183 cm' (your height).

- The students ask whatever questions they can think of which might elicit this answer. Write all these questions on the board in the right-hand column, inviting correction when necessary. Remain silent until one student asks a question which elicits the answer on the board, for example 'How tall are you?' '183 cm'.

- Repeat this process with another piece of information about yourself, until enough questions have been asked to form a fairly comprehensive questionnaire on the board. You may now choose to answer any of the other questions on the board.

- Finally, put the students into pairs. Ask them to interview each other, using the questions on the board, and to take notes.

- As homework, students can write a brief profile of their partner.

Three Answers

From answers to questions

Level	Pre-intermediate onwards
Activity type	Mingle/open space activity
Equipment/ Materials	Slips of paper

- On the board, write three pieces of information about yourself, for example the colour of your car, the age of your cat, and the name of your first husband/wife.

- The students ask whatever questions they can think of which might lead to these answers. Remain silent until one student asks a question which elicits the answer on the board, for example 'What colour is your car?' 'Red'.

- Give each student a piece of paper. On this piece of paper each student writes three different pieces of information about himself/herself.

- The students mingle and find a partner. They ask questions to elicit the answers on their partner's piece of paper.

- Finally, the students discuss what they have found out about each other.

Marketing Mix

A class consumer survey

Level	Pre-intermediate onwards
Activity type	Groupwork/mingle
Equipment/ Materials	None

- Divide the class into small groups. Choose one consumer product for each group, for example cars, portable stereos, bank accounts, women's magazines. Allocate a different product to each group in the class.

- Working within their groups, the students produce a questionnaire which they feel will help them to design the perfect product for the market represented by their school or college.

- When these questionnaires are complete, the students question the other students within the class or the school, in order to do a market research survey on their allocated product.

- They then return to their groups and form a description of a product that would best suit their own market.

- Finally, each group presents their ideas to the class.

Public Opinion Survey

Students produce a questionnaire to test public opinion in an English-speaking country

Level	Intermediate onwards
Activity type	Groupwork
Equipment/ Materials	Photocopies
Plus ...	A selection of newspapers (see below)

- Bring in a selection of newspapers. Ask the students to identify a current topic about which the general public will have strong opinions.

- Put the students into small groups and ask them to devise a questionnaire which is designed to gauge local public opinion on the chosen topic.

- Photocopy the questionnaires.

- The students go out in pairs to interview members of the public, using their questionnaires.

- Finally, they report back the results of their survey to the class.

Action to Be Taken

Give your students a say (in English)

Level	Pre-intermediate onwards
Activity type	Groupwork
Equipment/ Materials	None

- Select an issue within the school that the class can be expected to have some influence on, for example the position of computers in the library or the end-of-term party.

- Put the class into small groups and ask each group to produce a questionnaire which can be used within the school or college to find out people's views on this particular issue.

- Working in their groups, the students interview members of the school using their questionnaire.

- When they return to the classroom, the students discuss what they have found out.

- As a class, the students may then make recommendations to the member of staff responsible for that area of decision-making.

Notes and Queries

Genuine questions and answers throughout the course

Level	Elementary onwards
Activity type	Whole class; homework (optional)
Equipment/ Materials	Slips of paper
Plus ...	A 'question box' (see below)

- Set up a 'question box' in the classroom. Next to it, place slips of paper.

- During the course, the students write on the slips of paper any general knowledge questions that they would like to have answered, for example 'Why did dinosaurs become extinct?' 'How many films has Brad Pitt been in?'

- Empty the box every two weeks and distribute the questions amongst the students. Make sure that the students who originally wrote the questions do not receive the question slips that they themselves have written.

- The students use any resources available to find the answer to the questions that they have been given. This may be done as homework.

- Students then present questions and answers to the class.

Chain Questionnaire

Building a personalised questionnaire for each pair of students

Level	Elementary onwards
Activity type	Pairwork
Equipment/ Materials	None

- Put the students into pairs. Ask them to find three things that they have in common. Each pair should report their findings back to the class, for example Juan and Anna might say 'We've both been to Portugal', 'We both love Coca-Cola' and 'We both fight with our elder sisters.'

- When each pair has reported back, the class as a group decides what they would like to know more about for each pair of students – Juan and Anna's trips to Portugal, for example.

- Hand each pair of students a blank piece of paper. At the top of it they write their names and what the class would like to know more about.

- Each piece of paper is passed round. Each pair of students writes down any questions that they would like to ask and passes the sheet on. As each sheet is circulated, a questionnaire forms.

- Stop the activity after ten minutes. Each pair will have a questionnaire in front of them addressed to a different pair of students. They take it in turns to put the questions in front of them to the appropriate members of the class. The others listen.

Question-stem Questionnaire

Students produce a spontaneous oral questionnaire

Level	Elementary to Intermediate
Activity type	Pairwork
Equipment/ Materials	Photocopies
Plus ...	A questionnaire (see below)

- Produce a questionnaire for your students, consisting only of the first words of possible questions, as below, and make one copy for each student. What ... ? Where ... ? When ... ? Did ... ?

- Put the students into pairs. Ask them to find three things that they have in common. Each pair reports their findings back to the class, for example Juan and Anna say 'We've both been to Berlin' 'We both love Lou Reed' and 'We both fight with our elder sisters'.

- When each pair has reported back, the class as a group decides what they would like to know more about for each pair of students – Juan and Anna's trips to Berlin, for example.

- The other students ask questions about their trips. Each question must begin with one of the question words, for example 'Where did you stay?' Every time a student uses one of the question words, he or she places a tick next to it.

- This continues with each pair of students.

- Students then count their ticks and a winner is declared.

10

The Word Box

Make a word box for each class at the beginning of the course. This box will fill up with new lexical items that occur in the class and provide you with a valuable resource. Explain to your students that the box is a bank of all the words they will learn and practise. Use these activities frequently for lexical practice.

Choose a cardboard box with a lid and cover it with colourful paper. It should be quite big as it will fill up very quickly! Cut up pieces of durable card in advance. Cards can all be the same colour, or different. A new colour can be used to show when new students have come into the class, or a different colour can be used for each week. This will help you to decide how recent the vocabulary to be recycled should be. Colour-coding can provide a helpful topic guide if the course is topic-based. Alternatively, colour-code the cards according to verbs, nouns, phrasal verbs, adverbs, etc.

What can be put in the box? Not only individual words but also collocations, set expressions, idioms, phrasal verbs etc. Additional useful information that may be marked on the cards can include phonemic script, small drawings, opposites, (partial) synonyms, definitions, example phrases, and indication of register or connotation.

Students should not be encouraged to put all of these on the cards, but it is useful to make them aware of some of the possibilities.

At lower levels it can be useful to mark the stress patterns on the other side, using bubbles. This helps the student reading the word to pronounce it in recycling activities, and creates opportunities for pronunciation games.

Students enjoy being responsible for putting new words in the box. A class rota (daily/weekly) generally works well. Pair students up for this so that choosing the words for the box becomes a communicative activity in itself.

Hot Seat

Students elicit recent vocabulary from each other

Level	All levels
Activity type	Competitive activity/game
Equipment/ Materials	Word box and word cards

- Divide the class into small teams. One member of each team has their back to the board.

- A word is put on the board and each team has to get their team member to say the word by eliciting it, but without using mime. The first team to get the word gains a point.

- Change the 'guessers' after every three words. This can be a very lively game.

Points Word Stacks

Students compete to come up with recent vocabulary

Level	Pre-intermediate onwards
Activity type	Groupwork
Equipment/ Materials	Word box and word cards

- Divide the class into groups, and give each group the same number of words from the word box. These are placed face down in the middle of each group.

- One student picks up a card and then tries to elicit the word or phrase from the rest of the group. If this person doesn't know the word, the card is put on a separate pile of 'problem words'.

- When someone in the group says the word that the first student is trying to elicit, he or she gets the card, and this counts as one point.

- The next student then picks up a card and tries to elicit this word or phrase from the other members of the group. The game continues in this way.

- When all the groups have used the original stack of words, collect the 'problem words' from each group. Try to elicit each of these words from the whole class. Again, any student who says the word, gets the card. The student with the most cards (or points) in the class wins.

Group Word Stacks

Groups race to come up with recent vocabulary

Level	All levels
Activity type	Groupwork
Equipment/ Materials	Word box and word cards

- Divide the class into groups and give each group the same number of words from the word box. These should be placed face down in the middle of each group.

- One student picks up a card and then tries to elicit the word or phrase from the rest of the group. If this person doesn't know the word, they may look in their file, or in a dictionary.

- When someone in the group 'finds' the word, another student picks up a card and tries to elicit this word or phrase.

- The first group to get through their stack wins. Groups can then exchange stacks and start again.

Question Labels

Students ask questions to discover the mystery words

Level	Pre-intermediate onwards
Activity type	Mingle/open space activity
Equipment/ Materials	Word box and word cards; labels

- Select vocabulary from the class word box. You will need one card for each student in the class. Transfer each word onto a separate label.

- Ask the students to stand with their backs to you and place one label on each back. Allow the students to turn, mingle and examine each other's labels.

- Explain that the aim of the activity is to find out which word they have on their backs. They can only do this by asking yes/no questions, for example: 'Do you walk this way when you've had too much to drink?' (stagger)

- The students then mingle and ask questions, in order to discover the words on their backs.

- You may wish to choose words which belong to clearly-defined, and related, lexical groups, for example: ways of walking, ways of talking, and ways of looking. At the end of the activity, you can ask the students to stand in groups according to the lexical group in which they belong. The students may then discuss the differences of meaning within their groups.

Drawing Race

High-speed pictionary

Level	All levels
Activity type	Competitive activity/game
Equipment/ Materials	Word box and word cards; scrap paper

- Put the class into teams of three to five students. Give each team a pile of scrap paper and a pencil.

- Ask one student from each group to come to the front of the class. These are the 'drawers'. Show the drawers a word card from the class box.

- They run back to their teams, and draw the word in order to elicit it from other members of the team. The drawers are not permitted to talk. The first team to get the word gains one point.

- Change drawers and give them a new word. The game continues in this way. The team with the most points wins.

Variation

- Follow the same procedure as above for forming teams.

- Ask one student from each group to come to the front of the class. These are the mimes. Show the mimes a word card from the class box.

- They run back to their teams, and mime the word in order to elicit it from other members of the team. The 'mimes' are not permitted to talk. The first team to get the word gains one point.

- Change mimes and give them a new word. The game continues in this way. The team with the most points wins.

Card Trading

A co-operative activity in which students collect cards

Level	All levels
Activity type	Mingle/competitive activity
Equipment/ Materials	Word box and word cards

- Give each student in the class the same number of words from the word box. Ten to fifteen cards normally works well. Choose them at random.

- The students mingle and find a partner. In this case, Juan partners Mika.

- If Juan knows the word on the first card in his stack, he has to elicit it from Mika. If Mika says the word, she gets the card.

- If Juan does not know the word on the first card, he asks Mika what it means. If she can explain it satisfactorily, Mika gets the card.

- Mika then does the same with the first of her cards.

- After three or four minutes, ask all the students to change partners. The game continues in this way.

- The student with the most cards at the end of the activity is the winner.

Favourite Words

An imagination-stretching group writing activity

Level	Elementary onwards
Activity type	Pairwork
Equipment/ Materials	Word box and word cards

- Put the students into pairs, and give each pair a pile of cards from the word box.

- Ask them to choose their five 'favourite' words from their pile. This will involve a degree of revision and discussion.

- Once they have chosen their five words, they write a paragraph that includes all five.

- They then read the story/paragraph to the other pairs, pausing when they come to a 'favourite word', the other students have to guess which word they are about to read.

This is based on an activity in *Learner-Based Teaching* (Colin Campbell and Hanna Kryszewska, OUP).

Comparing Words

A short activity for revising comparatives

Level	Elementary to Intermediate
Activity type	Groupwork
Equipment/ Materials	Word box and word cards

- Put the students into small groups, and give each group twelve word cards picked at random.

- The students place these in front of them, face up. Working together, each group tries to produce as many sentences as they can which compare two of the words in front of them. Give them a time limit. While this is going on, circulate and help with accuracy.

- At the end of the allotted time, see which group has produced the most sentences. You may wish to ask each group to read out their most ridiculous comparison.

Continuouswordsearch

Studentswithscriptproblemstrytofindwordboundaries!

Level	Pre-intermediate onwards
Activity type	Whole class
Equipment/ Materials	Word box and word cards; photocopies; OHP (optional)
Plus ...	A word list (see below)

- Select words that you wish to revise from the word box. Write them as one continuous word and photocopy one for each student.

- The students then work to find the word boundaries. You may wish to show the answers on an OHT.

- Alternatively, you may wish to present the students with a more challenging list, in which the last letter of one word serves as the first letter of the subsequent word, for example 'teacherabbitelephonecstasyodel.'

Word Stress Game

Take the stress out of stress

Level	Beginner to Intermediate
Activity type	Groupwork
Equipment/ Materials	Word box and word cards
Plus ...	Word cards with stress patterns marked on the back (see the *Section Introduction*)

- Put the students into groups, and give each group a stack of cards with the words facing up.

- Ask them to organize the cards into groups which share the same stress patterns. When they are satisfied with their groupings, they turn the cards over to see whether they were right.

- The group that has made the fewest mistakes wins. The groups may then swap stacks and repeat the exercise.

Five Cards

Writing example sentences with target vocabulary is boring ... or is it?

Level	Pre-intermediate onwards
Activity type	Groupwork/ competitive activity
Equipment/ Materials	Word box and word cards

- Divide the class into small groups or teams. Give each team fifteen cards.

- Ask them to choose five cards with which they would like to test the other teams.

- The first group reads out the first of their target words. The other groups have one minute in which to write a sentence using this word. These sentences are then passed back to the team which has chosen the word.

- The second group reads out the first of their target words. Continue until each group or team has presented one word.

- Now explain the scoring system: three points for a sentence which uses the word appropriately or has no mistakes, two points for appropriate use and one mistake, one point for appropriate use but two or three mistakes, no points for four or more mistakes or which uses the word inappropriately.

- Put the score on the board. Continue until all the cards have been used.

Three Words

A simple activity that is more an exploration of grammar and collocation than a revision exercise

Level	All levels
Activity type	Pairwork/groupwork (optional)
Equipment/ Materials	Word box and word cards

- Select three words from the word box and write them on the board.

- Put the students into small groups or pairs. Their task is to produce a sentence containing the three words on the board. It should be grammatically correct and make sense. Give them a time limit.

- Display the sentences on an OHP or read them aloud.

- At lower levels award one point for each correct sentence. At higher levels award one point for the shortest plausible sentence.

11

Dictionaries

This section is concerned with the use of monolingual, or 'English-English,' dictionaries. Most of the major publishers offer a wide range. Monolingual dictionaries come in different sizes and vary in the features they offer.

These features may include phonemic transcriptions showing word stress, definitions pitched at different levels, and information on how the word is used to 'do things'. They may also offer information on grammar, collocation, connotation, as well as denotation, partial synonyms and antonyms. A number of dictionaries also provide guidance on register and social acceptability.

The activities in this section show the dictionary as an everyday tool in the language classroom, and also equip students with strategies needed for their own independent study. Activities cover familiarization with monolingual dictionaries, the use of dictionaries to diagnose student errors and expand errors, and the development of specific dictionary skills.

In this section, the activities assume the availability of a class set of dictionaries. The first part (*Familiarization*) helps students to get to know their way around a dictionary, and what it is capable of. The second part (*Problem Diagnosis*) shows them how to use a dictionary to help them with their individual language difficulties. The third part (*Practice Activities*) presents a variety of other dictionary activities.

Ordering Words

Introduce younger students and students who are not used to Roman script to the main ordering principle in dictionaries

Level	Beginner and Pre-intermediate
Activity type	Pairwork
Equipment/ Materials	Photocopies
Plus ...	A list of words (see below)

- Write, or if you wish to make it more difficult, dictate, a list of words, not in alphabetical order, for your students to put into the correct order. Adjust the level of difficulty according to the level of your students.

- Put the students in pairs. They work together and then use a dictionary to check their answers.

Compare Dictionaries

Help your students to discover what information they can find in a range of dictionaries – this will help them to make an intelligent choice

Level	Pre-intermediate onwards
Activity type	Pairwork
Equipment/ Materials	None
Plus ...	At least three different monolingual dictionaries and a list of words (see below)

- Give the students a range of dictionaries and a list of words. Ask them to compare how the words are dealt with in each dictionary and what information each dictionary gives them.

- Put the students into pairs. Working together, ask them to produce a table demonstrating the differences they have discovered.

Door-to-Door Dictionaries

An information-gap roleplay where the information exchanged helps the students as learners

Level	Pre-intermediate onwards
Activity type	Mingle/open space activity
Equipment/ Materials	None
Plus ...	At least three different monolingual dictionaries

- Put the students into two groups. The first group are consumers; as a group they discuss what they want from a dictionary. The second group are salespeople – give them time to look at their products and prepare their sales pitch.

- When they are ready, the students mingle, gathering information and trying to sell their products.

- At the end, the students decide which dictionary they would choose.

Pick a Page at Random

A quick filler when you have some students who have finished an activity before the others

Level	Elementary onwards
Activity type	Pairwork
Equipment/ Materials	None

- Put the students into pairs. Ask them to look at one page of the dictionary and try to remember as many words as they can.

- After they have had a few minutes to do this, one student tests the other student.

- Make sure that you use a dictionary that is relatively easy for your students.

Dictionary Page Diagnosis

An activity that helps students to diagnose their own language problems by using a dictionary

Level	Elementary onwards
Activity type	Pairwork
Equipment/ Materials	Photocopies
Plus ...	A mistakes sheet (see below)

- Collect some recent student errors, either written or spoken. Write these out as numbered sentences. Make sure that they are mistakes that can be corrected using the information in your class dictionary and write, next to each numbered sentence, the page number in the dictionary that will give the students the necessary information to correct the sentences.

- Give your students the photocopied mistakes sheet and ask them to work in pairs to correct the sentences.

Variation

- Follow the previous procedure, but this time do not give the page numbers in the dictionary. You may wish to underline problems in the sentences if you think that this is necessary.

False Friends Paragraph

Monolingual groups try to spot mistranslations

Level	Pre-intermediate onwards
Activity type	Pairwork
Equipment/ Materials	Photocopies
Plus ...	A mistakes sheet (see below)

- Produce a series of sentences, each of which contains an error based on a mistranslation of a word that appears to be the same, or similar, in both languages, for example 'She's so sensible: it's very easy to hurt her feelings.'

- Give your students the photocopied mistakes sheet and ask them to work in pairs to correct the sentences using monolingual dictionaries.

- When they have found all the mistakes, correct them as a class.

- Finally, ask the students to include the original words in an appropriate context, for example 'She's so sensible: she has her car serviced every six months.'

Particle Physics

'Think of' or 'think about' – why not use a dictionary to decide?

Level	Intermediate onwards
Activity type	Pairwork
Equipment/ Materials	Photocopies
Plus ...	A photocopied sheet (see below)

- Make a list of phrasal verbs and dependent prepositions that you wish to test your students on.

- Write ten sentences, each of which includes at least one example from your list, but get all the particles and prepositions wrong. Make one photocopy for each pair of students.

- Put the students into pairs. Working together the students try to correct them and then use dictionaries to check their answers.

New Words – Odd One Out

A puzzle best solved with the aid of a dictionary

Level	Elementary onwards
Activity type	Groupwork; pairwork (optional)
Equipment/ Materials	Slips of paper
Plus ..	Four slips of paper (see below)

- Take four slips of paper. On each slip write five words, one of which is the 'odd one out'. Be careful when doing this to set a puzzle which is appropriate to the level of your group and which can be answered using the information in your class dictionary. You may wish to make the task more demanding by using grammatical or phonemic criteria.

- Put the students into four groups. Give each group one of the slips of paper and a dictionary. Ask them to find the odd one out and to keep a record of their reasoning. Give them three or four minutes to do this.

- Circulate the slips of paper and repeat the procedure until all the groups have seen all the slips of paper.

- Finally compare the findings as a class.

New Words – Link Them

Don't just find out what they mean – put them in a context

Level	Elementary onwards
Activity type	Pairwork
Equipment/ Materials	None

- Choose five words which you think will be new to your class, and which you can imagine occurring in a single context, for example *spooky, haunted, creep* and *creak*.

- Divide the class into pairs and give each pair a dictionary. Write the words on the board, and explain that the aim of each pair is: firstly, to look up the words, checking both meaning and usage; and secondly, to write a short text which includes the words in any order.

- Each pair reads their story to the class.

Word Stress Match

Familiarize your students with how word stress is indicated in the dictionary

Level	Beginner to Pre-intermediate
Activity type	Pairwork
Equipment/ Materials	Photocopies
Plus ...	A list of words (see below)

- On a piece of paper write words of different stress patterns. Photocopy this for each pair of students.

- Put the students into pairs and ask each pair to group the words according to stress patterns.

- The students use the dictionaries to check their answers.

Chris Campbell's Activity

Teaching phrasal verbs can be problematic – why not get the students to do it?

Level	Pre-intermediate onwards
Activity type	Pairwork/groupwork (optional)
Equipment/ Materials	Slips of paper

- Take a maximum of ten slips of paper. On each slip of paper write a phrasal verb which you think will be unfamiliar to your class. These verbs may be unrelated, or they may have one verb, or particle, in common.

- Divide the class into pairs, or small groups if necessary. Give each pair one of the slips of paper and a monolingual dictionary. Ask them to look up their phrasal verb, choose a meaning that they think is useful, and write a short dialogue that contains their chosen use of the phrasal verb. Circulate and help if necessary.

- When all the pairs have completed their dialogues, ask the first pair to read theirs to the class. Ask the other students to identify the new phrasal verb and to say what they think it means in this context. The first pair can confirm or clarify as necessary. Record the phrasal verb, and the agreed use, on the board.

- The second pair read their dialogue and the process continues in the same way. Repeat the process until all the new phrasal verbs have been discussed and recorded.

- As homework the students can write an example sentence for each phrasal verb.

Spelling Match

A spelling/pronunciation/dictionary/ phonemic chart familiarization activity – what more do you want?

Level	Elementary to Intermediate
Activity type	Pairwork
Equipment/ Materials	Prepared cards

- Write words on one set of cards and their phonemic transcriptions on another. Mix them up, and ask the students to match them.

- They use dictionaries to check their answers.

- With stronger students, use difficult words, for example *toe, cough, although* and *kneel.*

12

The OHP

The OHP (overhead projector) is a wonderfully flexible classroom tool. It allows the teacher to make a body of text available to the whole class instantly and legibly, minimizing the time spent writing material on the board with their back to the class. It also provides a greater degree of control over the presentation of a text, through such techniques as masking, use of colour, overlays and using a series of OHTs (overhead transparencies). OHTs can be reused, so that your preparation time is put to best use, and can reduce the number of photocopies that are used in class. They are an extremely efficient way of giving answers to a wide variety of classroom and homework tasks.

Students often prefer them to the whiteboard for a number of reasons. OHTs may be photocopied, giving the students a written record which is the same as that used in the lesson. Many students find it difficult to write on a whiteboard. OHTs also allow them to produce a range of materials which can then be made available to the rest of the class. This is especially useful for class talks, displaying conclusions reached in group discussions, and class discussion of individual writing tasks.

OHPs help create an atmosphere of concentration and group focus. Visual images become infinitely stronger when projected in a darkened room. Roleplays, discussions and many group activities always seem to go better when the OHP is involved. OHPs are also very useful for 'staging a lesson'. They provide a clear break from whatever has preceded them.

Here we have tried to show the range of possibilities for the OHP. The first part (*Existing Text Techniques*) looks at ways in which OHPs can be used with a variety of existing texts such as advertisements, letters and songs, and provides a basic list of techniques that may be useful in a number of different situations. The second part (*Student Text Activities*) lists a number of activities that are based on student writing. The third part (*Other Activities*) lists various other activities that work well with the OHP.

Text Prediction

Level	All levels
Activity type	Whole class
Equipment/ Materials	OHP

- Reveal a photocopied OHT of a text, line by line. Encourage the students to predict what is 'coming next'.

- Focus: grammar, collocation and discourse and a variety of student skills.

Cut-up Lines

Level	All levels
Activity type	Whole class
Equipment/ Materials	OHP

- Cut up an OHT of a text, line by line. Place the lines at random on the OHP. Allow the students time to read the cut-up lines. The students negotiate in order to reconstruct the text. You may wish to give one student the responsibility of manipulating the text on the OHP.

- Focus: grammar, discourse, vocabulary and pronunciation (for songs).

Categorizing Words by Colour

Level	All levels
Activity type	Whole class
Equipment/ Materials	OHP; photocopies

- Give the students a photocopy of a text. Ask them to mark all the words of a particular category, either grammatical or lexical, on the text, working together. Check this, using coloured pens, on the OHT.

- Focus: word grammar, word sets.

Dialogue Prediction

Level	All levels
Activity type	Whole class
Equipment/ Materials	OHP

- Reveal the transcript of a dialogue line by line. Elicit as much about the characters and the context as you can, before moving on to the next line.

- Focus: social English, turn-taking.

Cut-up Paragraphs

Level	All levels
Activity type	Whole class
Equipment/ Materials	OHP

- Choose a text with more than six paragraphs. Make a photocopied OHT and cut between each paragraph. Place the paragraphs in the wrong order on the OHT and ask the students to read them for a few minutes. The students should then 'negotiate' the correct order of the text.

- Focus: discourse features, writing skills.

Editing a Text on the Whiteboard

Level	All levels
Activity type	Whole class
Equipment/ Materials	OHP

- Use a text that you wish to edit. Project this onto a whiteboard. Give one student a board pen and ask the other students to suggest amendments.

- Focus: punctuation, spelling, grammar, vocabulary.

100 Points Game

Competition-motivated students scrutinize each other's work

Level	Elementary onwards
Activity type	Competitive activity/game
Equipment/ Materials	OHP; scrap paper

- Organize the class into a maximum of four teams. Give each team a name. Write the names of the teams on the board and award each team 100 points. Tell the students that in the game they are going to play, they can both win points and lose them.

- Give each team scrap paper, an OHT, and an OHT pen. Tell them that they have two minutes to write a sentence which they all believe to be grammatically correct. At the end of two minutes they will have to transfer their sentence onto the OHT.

- Explain that everyone will then look at the sentence. If the other teams find a mistake in the sentence, they will lose as many points as there are words in the sentence. If the opposing teams cannot find a mistake they can ask you. If you are unable to see a mistake, the team's score remains unchanged. If you can find no mistakes, the team is awarded as many points as there are words in the sentence.

- Give the students the bad news. The sentence they write must begin with the word or phrase that you write on the board. Suggested words for lower levels: *If...When... Where... Who... Yesterday... Tomorrow...* and for higher levels: *Although... Despite... Since... Given... Having... Had...*

Error Correction Race

The question is, not who can make the most errors, but who can correct them?

Level	Elementary to Intermediate
Activity type	Competitive activity/game
Equipment/ Materials	OHP; different coloured board pens

- Produce an OHT of recent student errors, whether spoken or written. Put the students into a maximum of three teams and give each team a different coloured board pen. Put the teams at the back of the classroom.

- Project the OHT onto a whiteboard. The students take it in turns to race to the front of the class to correct any errors. Only one member of each team is allowed at the board at a time.

- Each correction gains the team one point, but if it is wrong the team loses two points.

Dictogloss

Heard fragments become complete texts

Level	Elementary onwards
Activity type	Groupwork
Equipment/ Materials	OHP; photocopies
Plus ...	A short text (see below)

- Choose a short narrative or descriptive text. Make a copy for each student.

- Now read the text aloud to the class at normal speed.

- Tell the students that you are going to read the same text again and that they should write down any keywords that they hear. Explain that you will read the text at the same speed as before, and that they should not attempt to write down every word.

- Read the text aloud for a second time. After you have done so, put the students into groups, and tell them that, together, they have to construct a text which includes the language that they have just recorded.

- Photocopy the completed texts onto an OHT and allow the class to read each text in turn.

- Give the students a copy of the original text to study.

Memory Game

A well-known party game sometimes called Kim's game

Level	Elementary onwards
Activity type	Pairwork/groupwork (optional)
Equipment/ Materials	OHP
Plus ...	An OHT (see below)

- You may wish to precede this task with a revision of relevant vocabulary, prepositions of place and the language of negotiation.

- Prepare an OHT showing an array of objects on a tray or desk.

- Project the OHT and allow the students to see the projection for a brief period of time, for example one minute.

- Then switch off the OHP, and the students, working in pairs or small groups, have to reconstruct the image they have seen. They can do this, either by drawing the items in the right place on a sheet of paper, or by writing the names of those objects in the position they remember seeing them.

- Finally project the OHT once more so that students can assess their performance.

- You may wish to follow this activity with any of the following: a mistakes session, a session on any area of language that the students found difficult, or a video recording of proficient English users doing the same task, possibly followed by further practice.

Getting Everything Wrong

Incompetent with technology? Make the most of it!

Level	Elementary onwards
Activity type	Whole class
Equipment/ Materials	OHP
Plus ...	An OHT with gapped instructions on how to use an OHP

- Place the OHP in a prominent position and ask whether everybody can see the text properly. Make sure that the machine is not switched on.

- Do everything wrong ...

- Don't plug in the OHP. Make sure that the lens is dirty, out of focus and aimed at the ceiling. Ensure that all the lights are on in the room, and that any curtains or blinds are open. Put the OHT on upside down and back to front. Put the OHP too far, or too close to the board, to be able to focus it successfully. Stand in front of the projector.

- Once your students start to point and gesticulate in order to give you instructions, ask them to sit on their hands, and do exactly what they say – even if it is wrong.

- When, finally, the whole class is able to read the OHT, ask the students to fill in the gaps in the model instructions.

- This activity also works well with cassette recorders, VHS machines, camcorders and computers.

Out of Focus Pictures

An enjoyable way of presenting or recycling modal verbs for deduction

Level	Elementary to Intermediate
Activity type	Whole class
Equipment/ Materials	OHP
Plus ...	OHTs (photocopied or drawn) of recognizable places, people or objects

- Before you project the OHT to the students, ensure that it is out of focus. Project the out of focus image and invite the students to guess what it is, for example: 'It might be an elephant.'

- Gradually bring the image into focus, encouraging students to reappraise constantly, for example: 'It can't be an elephant; it hasn't got four legs. It might be the headmaster.'

- Repeat with other images.

Back to Picture Questions

Students love the opportunity to wrongfoot you – make them work to achieve this!

Level	All levels
Activity type	Competitive activity/game (optional)
Equipment/ Materials	OHP
Plus ...	An OHI (see below)

- Choose a picture that will elicit the language that you wish to practise. It may be a picture with a lot going on, for example to practise the present continuous at a low level. It may be a photograph of a landscape to elicit the language of mood and environment at a higher level. Almost any picture may be of value.

- Project the image so that everybody can see it. Look at the picture yourself for, say, 30 seconds and then stand so that your back is to it. The students should then ask you as many questions as they can in order to test your memory of it. They, of course, are practising their English.

- You can make this into a game by telling the students that their aim is to get you to make, for example, ten mistakes in three minutes.

- You may wish to extend this activity by asking a student to take your place, with a new picture. Alternatively put the class into pairs or groups, and get them to do the activity themselves.

Where Are They?

Children's books often have 'Spot the ...' pictures – use them.

Level	Beginner to Pre-intermediate
Activity type	Pairwork
Equipment/ Materials	OHP
Plus ...	A 'Spot the ...' picture (see below)

- Photocopy a picture where students have to find a number of hidden objects or animals onto an OHT. Project it to the class.

- Put the students into pairs. Tell them to work together to find the hidden objects as quickly as they can, without pointing at the board, for example: 'Look! There's one in the slipper under the chair on the right.'

- Using an OHP ensures that the students have to use language to locate each of the objects. This method also works well with 'Spot the difference' pictures.

Picture Story Prediction

Motivating preparation, using a variety of tenses, for producing narratives

Level	Pre-intermediate onwards
Activity type	Pairwork/groupwork (optional); homework (optional)
Equipment/ Materials	OHP
Plus ...	A picture story (see below)

- Select a picture story with a maximum of eight to ten pictures. (Useful sources are teenage magazines or newspaper strips.) Photocopy it onto an OHT.

- Place the OHT on the machine and mask everything except the first picture. Switch on the OHP. Encourage the students to describe the picture and create as detailed a context as possible for it. Then, ask them to predict what happens next. Gather as many ideas as you can, encouraging debate where possible.

- Reveal the next picture in the story. Again, ask the students to describe the situation before predicting what happens next.

- Continue in the same way, revealing each picture one by one. After the third or fourth picture, ask your students to tell the story so far, placing the events in the past.

- Ask the students, either in class or at home, to write the story so far, and to conclude it themselves.

- Show the students the complete picture story and compare the different endings.

13

Computers

Computers have a number of distinct advantages over pen and paper for certain activities. They are particularly suitable for process writing activities, where texts are edited and redrafted. On computers, the script is always legible. Mistakes can be corrected tidily. Words and text can be moved easily (using 'cut and paste' or 'drag and drop'). This not only helps with student editing, but also makes reordering text exercises more natural, with a more polished final result.

Incomplete text may be saved on a computer, which means that it is not always necessary to finish a writing activity within a lesson, as it may easily be retrieved afterwards. Similarly, any material that you produce for the computer may be reused ad infinitum, and may also be quickly and easily altered for specific classes. It is possible to make printed copies of student-created work, which will not have any of the signs of the intensive correcting and redrafting that will have gone into it.

The nature of the computer monitor means that many group writing activities become easier on the computer. Students may point to the text, and all of them can see it at the same time (four is about the maximum number of students that you may wish to use for an activity of this type).

Students who are too shy to become fully involved in classroom activities or those who enjoy using technology will also like working on the computer.

Computers are particularly useful in self-access centres. Some of these activities may be adapted for self-access. But there are also an increasing number of purpose-made programs and CD-ROMs, DVD-ROMs and websites that are excellent for encouraging learner autonomy. Make a student log available when you have programs of this type available.

In this section we concentrate on three of the most basic tools available to the teacher who has a computer at his or her disposal: wordprocessing, e-mail and the popular text reconstruction program Storyboard.

Gapless Gaps

In normal gapped exercises, the students have to find the words to fill in the gaps. Why not also make them find the gaps themselves?

Level	All levels
Activity type	Whole class
Equipment/ Materials	Single/multiple computers (optional)
Plus ...	A text (see below)

- Choose a text and take out one group of words from it. These could be verbs, articles, prepositions or pronouns. Do not indicate where the words are missing.

- Ask the students to complete the text.

- As a variation, try taking out all the punctuation. You may wish to make all the words lower case (this can be done automatically by most wordprocessors).

Free Writing

Use computers to encourage descriptive writing

Level	Pre-intermediate onwards
Activity type	Pairwork/groupwork
Equipment/ Materials	Single/multiple computers

- Do this activity after you have done some work on descriptive writing in class.

- Put the students into pairs or small groups, and put each group in front of a computer.

- Start dictating the beginning of a narrative. For example 'You are in a house that you have never been into before. You walk into the room. It is absolutely extraordinary … Describe the room.' Give the students time to write a description of the room, working in pairs.

- Continue the story: 'As you are looking around the room, a most unusual person walks in …' Give the students time to write a description of the person, working in pairs.

- Continue the story: 'The person looks at me and starts a conversation … Write the dialogue.' Give the students time to write the dialogue.

- Ask the students to write a narrative, which may or may not begin in the same way as you have begun, and which links all three elements that you have introduced.

- At the end of the lesson, compare the stories.

Complete an Incomplete Text

Students take up where the story leaves off

Level	Elementary onwards
Activity type	Whole class
Equipment/ Materials	Single/multiple computers (optional)
Plus ...	A text (see below)

- This technique works well with letters, stories and dramatic monologues. Give your students the first part of a text on screen. Ask them to predict the content of the remainder of the text, and then to complete it in their own words. If the text is a letter, they should continue in the same register and tone.

- Print out the students' texts and compare them with the original.

Incomplete Story

Students take up where their classmates' story leaves off

Level	Elementary to Upper-intermediate
Activity type	Pairwork/groupwork
Equipment/ Materials	Multiple computers
Plus ...	A story (see below)

- Give your students the first part of a story on screen. Ask them to continue the story in their own words, working in pairs or small groups.

- After five minutes, ask each pair or group to move to the next computer and to continue the story that they find there.

- Repeat this as often as you wish.

Expanding Sentence

A testing, puzzle-like activity

Level	Pre-intermediate onwards
Activity type	Groupwork
Equipment/ Materials	Multiple computers

- Provide students with a simple sentence on screen, for example: 'I gave the homework to my teacher.'

- Put the students into groups. Each student should take it in turns to suggest a single word addition to the existing sentence, for example: 'I gave the homework to my *English* teacher.' Each time a new word is added, the group has to decide whether the sentence is still grammatical. You may be asked to adjudicate.

- In this way the original sentence might become 'Sighing deeply, I dutifully gave the unbelievably difficult homework to my unusually tall, dark, handsome English teacher boyfriend.'

- A brief story outline can also be expanded a similar way. The students should add either a single word, or groups of words, when it is their turn.

Using the Spellchecker

A spellchecker can be quite a blunt instrument – or a fine one

Level	Elementary onwards
Activity type	Whole class
Equipment/ Materials	Single/multiple computers (optional)
Plus ...	A text (see below)

- Produce a text with a large number of spelling mistakes, also include some wrong word mistakes i.e. words which are spelt correctly but are not correct in the context, for example: 'Hear's there money' or 'Discreet skills practise.'

- The students should use the spellcheck facility to correct the text. They will need to decide between a number of alternative spellings offered. They will also need to correct a number of spellings that the spellchecker cannot find.

Reordering Sentences

Order out of chaos?

Level	Pre-intermediate onwards
Activity type	Whole class
Equipment/ Materials	Single/multiple computers (optional)
Plus ...	A text (see below)

- Use the mouse, or 'cut and paste,' to rearrange the sentences in a text. You may wish only to move some sentences, and keep the existing paragraphing; or you may wish to lose the paragraphs as well.

- Ask the students to 're-assemble' the text.

Error Annotations

Most wordprocessors have an 'annotation' command

Level	Elementary onwards
Activity type	Pairwork/groupwork (optional)
Equipment/ Materials	Single/multiple computers (optional)
Plus ...	A different text on-screen for each computer

- Choose texts that are at an appropriate level for your students and have each text on-screen. Put the students into pairs or small groups, and put each group in front of a computer.

- Ask each group of students to make a list of the errors that they make most frequently. Give them a few minutes to do this.

- Ask them to amend the text so that it now includes a number of their 'favourite' errors, as many as they would like.

- Ask each group to move to a different computer. Tell them to try to spot the errors in the text that they are reading. For each error they should insert an annotation. This annotation should indicate the type of errror that has been introduced (for example, spelling, punctuation, verb tense, wrong word).

- Ask each group to move to a different computer again. This time they should try to correct the error within the annotation window. If they think that the annotation is incorrect, they should indicate this.

- Finally, ask each group to return to their original computer and check the text on-screen.

Amateur Typists

Nobody can type perfectly!

Level	Elementary onwards
Activity type	Pairwork/groupwork (optional)
Equipment/ Materials	Multiple computers; photocopies
Plus ...	A text (see below)

- Choose a text which contains problematic spellings and punctuation.

- Put the students into groups and seat each group around a computer. Ask one student in each group to be the 'typist.'

- Dictate the text at a speed that is perhaps a little faster than the speed at which most of your students can type comfortably.

- When you have finished the dictation, ask each group to move to a new computer, where they work to correct the poorly-typed, and possibly incomplete, text.

- Finally, read the text again, or give the students a printed copy, to enable them to check.

Travel Agents

Travel in cyberspace or just in your students' imaginations

Level	Elementary onwards
Activity type	Pairwork/groupwork (optional)
Equipment/ Materials	Multiple/networked computers (optional)
Plus ...	Travel brochures (see below)

- Collect two travel brochures from two different holiday companies. Ideally they should be from similar, but rival companies.

- Divide the class into four groups. Give two of the groups the brochures and tell them that they represent the two travel companies. Tell the two other groups that they are would-be holidaymakers looking for a good deal.

- Ask the two travel companies to familiarize themselves with their brochures and products. Ask the tourists to discuss where they would like to go and what sort of holiday they would like. You may wish to give them a budget and a map.

- When you feel the groups are prepared, ask the tourists to e-mail the holiday companies in order to negotiate their holiday. The travel companies should do their best to sell their own products; the tourists should try to get the best deal.

- This activity may be done with more groups. If so, it becomes even more demanding.

E-mail Roleplays

Get real – get wired!

Level	Pre-intermediate onwards
Activity type	Whole class
Equipment/ Materials	Networked computers
Plus ...	An activity (see below)

- Use e-mail as part, or all, of a roleplay activity. You can use it to establish a relationship before characters meet, for example an exchange of letters before a business meeting; and you can use it as the focus of the activity itself, for example the resolution of a difficult problem by correspondence.

Spoilt Brats

A roleplay that may be a little too realistic for some students

Level	Pre-intermediate onwards
Activity type	Pairwork/groupwork
Equipment/ Materials	Networked computers; multiple computers (optional)

- Put the students into groups of six. If this is not possible, it's easy to create extra roles. Divide each group into pairs and seat each pair at a computer. The three pairs must be able to communicate by e-mail.

- In each group of six, one pair is to play a couple who have sent their difficult children abroad, the second pair is to play their teenagers, and the third pair are the director of the school and the children's class teacher.

- The roleplay begins and the pairs busily email each other. The picture is confusing: the parents hear of nothing but hard work from their loved ones – but the school is painting a different picture. Can the situation be resolved?

- Allow the students to take the roleplay in any direction they like. The parents may decide to board a plane and sort things out on foreign soil – with no screen to hide behind; or the children may be expelled from the school.

- Alternatively, this roleplay may be done using postcards and letters, with the teacher acting as postperson.

Mistakes Text

Storyboard as a helping hand to accuracy

Level	All levels
Activity type	Whole class
Equipment/ Materials	Single/multiple computers (optional); photocopies
Plus ...	A text (see below)

- Type out a text that is full of mistakes on your wordprocessor. There may be problems of spelling, vocabulary or grammar on it. Print this out for your students. Type the corrected version of the text into Storyboard.

- Give the students the printed version and ask them to reconstruct a correct version, using Storyboard

Reconstructing Directions

From map to text via Storyboard

Level	Elementary onwards
Activity type	Whole class
Equipment/ Materials	Single/multiple computers (optional); photocopies
Plus ...	A text (see below)

- Type into Storyboard the directions from one place to another. Give the students a copy of a map or a plan with the places marked, and ask them to reconstruct the text.

Register Transformation

Challenge higher-level students with a shift in tone and register

Level	Upper-intermediate and Advanced
Activity type	Whole class
Equipment/ Materials	Single/multiple computers (optional); photocopies
Plus ...	Two texts (see below)

- Type one half of an existing register transformation exercise into Storyboard. Photocopy the other part for your students. Using the information from their photocopies, they should work to reconstruct the parallel text in a different register.

- This is a very demanding exercise, and may be done as revision after intensive work on the texts.

Storyboard Dictations

Storyboard as spellcheck

Level	All levels
Activity type	Whole class
Equipment/ Materials	Single/multiple computers (optional)
Plus ...	A text (see below)

- Dictate a text with a number of problem spellings to the students. They should write it down on paper. They then type their corrected text into Storyboard to check the spelling.

- This may be done on a word processor with a spellchecker, but this will need a great deal more teacher supervision.

Picture Stories

They say a picture tells a thousand words

Level	Pre-intermediate onwards
Activity type	Whole class
Equipment/ Materials	Single/multiple computers (optional); photocopies
Plus ...	A picture story and a text (see below)

- Select a picture story with a maximum of eight to ten pictures. Useful sources are teenage magazines or newspaper strips. Make one copy for each computer that you have. Create a story that follows the sequence of pictures and type the text into Storyboard.

- Give each group of students one of the photocopies, and ask them to reconstruct the story, using Storyboard.

Incomplete Dictation

Computer gap-fill

Level	Pre-intermediate onwards
Activity type	Whole class
Equipment/ Materials	Single/multiple computers (optional)
Plus ...	A text (see below)

- Dictate a story to the students but miss out all the verbs. The students should type the text into Storyboard as you dictate. They then have to complete the story by choosing the correct verbs.

- This technique tests the students' knowledge of vocabulary, collocation and grammar.

14

The Radio

It is possible to pick up stations which broadcast in English in almost every part of the world. The most famous are probably the BBC World Service and the Voice of America. These stations transmit a variety of programmes, such as news, sport, soap operas, pop music, youth programmes and specific programmes for learners of English.

These stations can be used in the classroom as a current, authentic source of listening material, or by individual learners as part of their own learning programme.

Activities in this section use live radio as a source for roughly-tuned input or a way of getting immediate information on topics the students are interested in. Radio can also be used as a basis for discussion and role-play, raising students' awareness of the phonological features of English and helping them to predict what a speaker is about to say, using linguistic clues.

Station Cruising 1

A familiarization activity for complete beginners

Level	Beginner
Activity type	Whole class
Equipment/ Materials	None
Plus ...	A radio

- Take a radio into class and search the airwaves for foreign language channels. When you come across either songs or speech in any language other than that of the students' own mother tongue(s), pause. Ask the students 'Which language is being spoken?'

- If the language is English, ask if they can tell whether it's American English, British English or any other form of English. Allow them to listen to any English channels for a short time. Then, before continuing your search, ask if they heard anything familiar. These might be the names of places, people or simply words similar to words in their own language.

- Repeat this activity occasionally as the course progresses.

Station Cruising 2

A more challenging familiarization activity

Level	Pre-intermediate onwards
Activity type	Pairwork
Equipment/ Materials	None
Plus ...	A radio

- Take a radio into class and trawl the airwaves for English language programmes. When you find one, stay tuned for a minute or two. Then switch off the radio. Ask the students what kind of radio programme they think they were listening to.

- When a clear picture has emerged, if necessary with your help, switch the radio back on (hoping that the programme hasn't changed!) and listen for a further two or three minutes, taking notes.

- Switch off the radio. Put the students into pairs, and ask them to compare notes on the excerpt that they have been listening to.

How many Stories?

A gentle introduction to the news in English

Level	Elementary and Pre-intermediate
Activity type	Pairwork
Equipment/ Materials	Single cassette player
Plus ...	A radio news broadcast (see below)

- Choose a fairly briskly-paced news broadcast, which will inevitably be too difficult for your students.

- Put the students into pairs, and ask them to brainstorm anything that is likely to be in that day's international news.

- Tell them that you are going to play them a news summary in English. Their task is very simple: they have to tell you, at the end of the broadcast, how many stories there were today in the news. Play the news and discuss it as a class.

- Play the news again, this time asking the students to note down the subject of each news story.

Who, What, Where, Why, When?

A standard-format question sheet that can be used both in class, and in a self-access centre

Level	Elementary onwards
Activity type	Pairwork
Equipment/ Materials	Single cassette player; photocopies
Plus ...	A radio news broadcast and a question form (see below)

- Choose a fairly briskly-paced news broadcast. Produce a form with columns headed *who, what, where, why* and *when*, and numbers down the left-hand side for each item in the news broadcast.

- Put the students into pairs, and ask them to brainstorm anything that is likely to be in that day's international news. They should listen to the news, cross off any items that were not mentioned and add the rest to their list.

- Hand out the question forms. The students listen to the news again and try to complete all the information required. With lower-level students you may wish them to work together in pairs again to complete the forms.

Pauses

'the two leaders met for ...'

Level	Pre-intermediate onwards
Activity type	Whole class
Equipment/ Materials	Single cassette player
Plus ...	A radio broadcast (see below)

- Record a broadcast that has many set phrases, collocations, idioms – even clichés! News programmes, and interviews with politicians, usually work well.

- Play it to your class, pausing whenever you think that your students should be able to complete the phrase, for example: 'the two leaders met for ...'. Discuss possible phrase endings and then continue the tape.

- You can use this to practise not only vocabulary, but also grammar, for example verb forms.

Trailer Chat

We all make decisions like this every day

Level	Pre-intermediate onwards
Activity type	Groupwork
Equipment/ Materials	Multiple cassette players
Plus ...	Three radio excerpts (see below)

- Record three trailers for forthcoming radio programmes onto three separate tapes. These often consist of a brief summary, information on the time that they are going to be broadcast, and an excerpt from the programme itself.

- Divide the class into three groups. Give each group a cassette-recorder and a different trailer. Place the groups at a distance from one another. Tell each group to listen to the trailer for their programme, and be prepared to describe it to the students in the other groups. Each group may listen to their own recording as many times as they like.

- Put the students into groups of three, with at least one student from each group. Ask them to describe their programme to the other members of the group. When they have done this, they decide together which programme they would like to listen to.

Rapid Information Listening

'and the highest of this week's climbers is...'

Level	Pre-intermediate onwards
Activity type	Whole class
Equipment/ Materials	Single cassette player
Plus ...	A radio broadcast (see below)

- Certain regular news broadcasts make good material for listening-for-specific information exercises. Examples of this type of broadcast are: the top 40 hit list, sports updates, or stock and share prices. Choose one that suits the interests of your class.

- Record it regularly and follow the ups and downs of the real world.

Good Interviewer?

Did the interviewer find out what your students want to know?

Level	Pre-intermediate onwards
Activity type	Pairwork/groupwork (optional)
Equipment/ Materials	Single cassette player
Plus ...	A radio broadcast (see below)

- Record a radio interview with a famous person, for example Arnold Schwarznegger.

- Tell your students that they are about to listen to an interview with Arnold Schwarznegger. Put them into pairs or small groups and ask them to write any questions that they would like to hear answered.

- Play the interview. The students should tick any questions which have been answered.

- Finally, the students tell the class which of their questions remained unanswered.

Requests and Competitions

Can your students win that holiday in the Bahamas?

Level	Elementary onwards
Activity type	Pairwork/groupwork (optional)
Equipment/ Materials	Single cassette player
Plus ...	A radio broadcast (see below)

- There are a lot of competitions in the youth programmes on the radio and there are also music programmes which invite requests. Record one of these.

- Play it to your class, and encourage the students, in pairs or groups, to enter for the competition that they have just heard about; or to request a record, saying why they want to hear it.

14

TV and Video

Many English language teachers now have access to TV and video recorders. Many schools keep recordings of programmes* taken directly off-air, as well as commercial videos designed for language learners. In this section we are chiefly concerned with using off-air recordings, including news programmes, documentaries, dramas, pop programmes and chat shows. Students and teachers alike have mixed feelings about the role of video in language-learning. Some students might see a video lesson as a 'soft option' whereas others may see it as a bewildering or even threatening listening exercise. Some teachers feel a degree of professional guilt about using the video in class and tend to overburden students with lengthy 'as you listen' comprehension questions and checklists.

On the other hand, most students enjoy using what is probably the primary means of communication in the modern world – television. This gives the teacher a classroom tool that comes from the real world, and towards which most students feel a great deal of goodwill. The visual aspect of video can be used to support learners by providing a context, as well as a guide to meaning. If this relationship is exploited positively, students can be supported in their exposure to a valuable authentic source, and given a great deal of confidence as English language users.

This section is divided into two parts: *Techniques and Resources* and *Activities*. In the first part we look at a variety of basic techniques that can be used with almost any video. We also offer a number of ideas for using less conventional resources, such as subtitled films. The second part comprises group activities which can be used with a variety of students and types of off-air recording. They involve intensive and extensive listening activities and use the techniques listed in the first part.

* When using material of this kind, always check the copyright regulations. These may vary from country to country.

Channel-hopping

Level	All levels
Activity type	Whole class
Equipment/ Materials	Single VHS player and TV

- Use the remote-control to drop in on different English language TV channels.

- Use this for language familiarization and roughly-tuned input. The students viewing the decontextualized excerpts can use any clues in order to form a picture of the type of TV programme being shown.

Picture Down, Sound Up

Level	All levels
Activity type	Whole class
Equipment/ Materials	Single VHS player and TV

- Show the video to the students with the screen covered, or the picture blacked out, but with the sound at normal volume.

- Use this to ask the students to anticipate what they think is on the screen, for example description of people or of settings. This works well with soundtracks that have dialogue or distinctive music.

Play/Fast Forward View

Level	All levels
Activity type	Whole class
Equipment/ Materials	Single VHS player and TV

- Show the video at high speed, with no sound.

- Use this to remind the students of what they have just seen, or allow some students to preview the remainder of a story in order to create an information gap.

Using the Pause Button

Level	All levels
Activity type	Whole class
Equipment/ Materials	Single VHS player and TV

- Use the pause button to freeze-frame the picture.

- Use this to create an opportunity for discussion of what has just happened, what is going to happen and a detailed description of what is on the screen at the moment.

Sound Down, Picture Up

Level	All levels
Activity type	Pairwork (optional)
Equipment/ Materials	Single VHS player and TV; multiple VHS players and TVs (optional)

- Show the video to the students with the volume set at zero.

- Use this to elicit language from the students that is related to the context and that may be used in the dialogue.

- The students can also provide voiceovers for a scene, either before or after watching it.

- They may create an English soundtrack for a non-English video, for example 'dubbing' English instructions onto a cookery programme.

- The students may provide a commentary to what is happening on the screen.

Jigsaw Sound and Picture

Level	All levels
Activity type	Pairwork/groupwork
Equipment/ Materials	Single VHS player and TV; multiple VHS players and TVs (optional)

- Allow one group of students to hear the soundtrack but not to see the picture, while the other group sees the picture but doesn't hear the soundtrack.

- Use this as an information gap activity.

Front-to-back Students

Level	All levels
Activity type	Pairwork
Equipment/ Materials	Single VHS player and TV

- Seat the students in pairs so that one student can see the screen and the other cannot. Turn the sound down if there is dialogue.

- This creates a genuine real-time information gap activity.

Spotting Signs

Level	All levels
Activity type	Whole class
Equipment/ Materials	Single VHS player and TV

- Get students to read any on-screen English, for example street signs, shop names, advertised hoardings, notices.

Subtitles in the Mother Tongue

Level	All levels
Activity type	Whole class
Equipment/ Materials	Single VHS player and TV

- If you have English language videos with subtitles in the students' mother tongue, use these to build student confidence. Play the video with the sound down, then play the video again with the sound up, but covering the subtitles.

Group Out, Group In

Level	All levels
Activity type	Pairwork/groupwork
Equipment/ Materials	Single VHS player and TV; multiple VHS players and TVs (optional)

- Put the class into two groups and create an information gap.

- This can be done in different ways. You can show one group of students a section of video that the other group has not seen. You can show one group the picture and play the other group the soundtrack, as mentioned in an earlier activity. Or you can show each group a different video or a different part of the same video.

The Film of the Novel

Level	All levels
Activity type	Whole class
Equipment/ Materials	Single VHS player and TV

- This activity works if you are able to compare a video with the book that it is based on; this may be your class reader or an authentic text. Many readers are adaptations of novels that have been made famous by recent Hollywood releases.

Subtitles in English

Level	All levels
Activity type	Whole class
Equipment/ Materials	Single VHS player and TV

- If you have foreign language videos with English subtitles, use these as reading practice for your students. You may wish to develop this idea if the video is in your students' mother-tongue.

Back-to-back Adverts

Many advertisements are oblique, creating a puzzle for your students

Level	Pre-intermediate onwards
Activity type	Pairwork
Equipment/ Materials	Single VHS player and TV
Plus ...	A recording of TV advertisements (see below)

• Record a series of TV advertisements. Ideally these should be ones where the product advertised becomes obvious only towards the end of the advertisement.

• Put the class into pairs and seat them so that one student can see the screen and the other cannot. Tell them that the students facing the screen are going to see a TV commercial and that they should describe exactly what they see to their partners.

• Play the first advertisement with the sound down, pausing where necessary to give the students a chance to describe what is happening. Stop the video before the product being advertised becomes clear. Ask any of the students who have not seen the screen what they think the commercial is for, and ask them to give reasons.

• Play the video so that all the students can see it, this time with the sound up. Discuss the language and images used before moving on to another commercial.

Vocabulary Concepts

An activity to make your students really listen

Level	Pre-intermediate onwards
Activity type	Pairwork
Equipment/ Materials	Single VHS player and TV; photocopies
Plus ...	A recording of a drama or a documentary and a vocabulary sheet (see below)

• Produce a vocabulary sheet with about fifteen words that are used in the video. Write the words down the centre of the page with space between them. Photocopy one for each pair of students in the class.

• Put the students into pairs and give each pair a vocabulary sheet. Go through the words with the class, discussing meanings and possible contexts for them.

• Play the video. Tell the students that they can look at their sheets, but that there is no need to write anything at this stage.

• After you have played the video, tell the students to try to recall the contexts in which the words were used. They should work in pairs. Tell them to write what they can remember next to the word on the sheet. This may be a spoken context, or simply what was happening on-screen at the time.

• Finally, the students pool their information. You can produce a written record of the contextualized words on the board.

But What Are They Thinking?

So much in life remains unsaid – or does it?

Level	Pre-intermediate onwards
Activity type	Groupwork (optional)
Equipment/ Materials	Single VHS player and TV; photocopies
Plus ...	A recording of a film or drama (see below)

• Choose a psychologically interesting scene from a film or drama which the students have already seen in class and which involves two or more characters. Show this scene to the students, and deal with any problems of comprehension or vocabulary.

• Put the students into groups with as many students as there are characters in the scene. Some students may have to double up. Ask each student to take on the role of one character in the scene. Tell them that they are going to express what each character is thinking.

• Play the scene again, pausing regularly when one of the characters has just finished speaking. While the video is paused, the students 'speak the minds' of their characters, expressing their feelings, thoughts and frustrations.

Building up to the News

A confidence-building introduction to an often daunting listening task

Level	Pre-intermediate onwards
Activity type	Whole class
Equipment/ Materials	Single VHS player and TV; photocopies
Plus ...	A recording of the news

- Take a recording of a TV news broadcast and choose two items which feature plenty of information, for example diagrams, photographs and footage. Make a list of words that are essential to an understanding of the broadcast. Photocopy one for each student.

- Show the two news items to the students with the sound turned down. After each item, ask the students to discuss, in groups, what they think the reports are about. Pool their conclusions.

- Hand out the vocabulary lists and deal with any problems of comprehension.

- Ask the students to work again, in their groups, and to use the keywords that they may have been given in order to try and reconstruct the story. At higher levels, this may be a speaking activity. At lower levels, appoint one of the students in each group as 'scribe', and ask them to produce their own news report.

- Finally, show the students the two items with the sound turned up, and compare with the students' own ideas.

They Do What?

'It's life, Jim ... but not as we know it.'

Level	Elementary onwards
Activity type	Groupwork
Equipment/ Materials	Single VHS player and TV
Plus ...	A recording (see below)

- Choose a video clip that is quintessentially English or American. A good example of this might come from an English soap opera like *Eastenders*. In order to complete this activity, your students do not need to understand all, or indeed any, of the dialogue.

- View the excerpt as a class and deal with any problems of comprehension, if you wish to.

- If you have a monolingual class, put your students into small groups and ask them to write sentences describing any differences between what they saw or heard, and life in their own country.

- If you have a multilingual class, put your students into small multilingual groups and ask them to discuss the differences between what they saw or heard and life in their own countries.

Putting Words Into Mouths

Conversation has stopped – can your students continue it?

Level	Elementary onwards
Activity type	Pairwork
Equipment/ Materials	Single VHS player and TV
Plus ...	A recording of two people speaking (see below)

- Choose a video clip that features two people having a conversation. At lower levels, this may be two people meeting for the first time or a shopkeeper and a customer. At higher levels the clip may be of a more complex relationship, or a more dramatic situation.

- Decide how much of the clip you wish to show in order to set the scene. With lower levels the clues may be entirely visual and you might begin with a single frozen frame. Start the video.

- Pause the video and ask the students to guess what the actors are going to say. Discuss their ideas, play the next few seconds of the clip and compare.

- Put the students into pairs. Play a few more seconds of the video. Pause it and the students continue the dialogue as they think it will progress.

- Play them a little more of the clip and ask them again to continue the dialogue from this new starting point.

- Continue this as you wish. To complete the activity, show the students the complete conversation.

Video Diary

They may be hard to watch, but they're even harder to make!

Level	Elementary onwards
Activity type	Groupwork
Equipment/ Materials	Single VHS player and TV
Plus ...	A camcorder

- Get the class to make a video diary. If you have a large class, split it into groups, and ask each group to agree to cover a different aspect of school life, for example lessons, lunch break, sports.

- The groups plan both what they are going to film and what they are going to say. They take it in turns to use the camcorder, and then edit the video together, if this is possible.

- The video can be shown to other classes or sent to an 'exchange school' in England or America, who may in turn produce their own video diary for **your** students.

Student News

'... and now over to our overseas correspondent ...'

Level	Pre-intermediate onwards
Activity type	Groupwork
Equipment/ Materials	Single VHS player and TV
Plus ...	A camcorder and a recording of a news broadcast (see below)

- Watch the news broadcast and discuss the language, focusing on journalistic phrases such as '... and now over to our overseas correspondent ...'.

- Tell the students that they are going to make a news broadcast, using themselves as subjects: school sports results, friendships breaking up, the everyday stuff of school life.

- Put the class into groups. Ask one group to be the newsroom team (i.e. newsreader, director and cameraperson) and ask each of the other groups to find a story which will make a good news item. Give the groups enough time to script their story as well as do any research. Meanwhile, the newsroom team should circulate to find out which stories are brewing.

- When the class is ready, all the news items are filmed with appropriate links.

Ad People

Turn an evening pastime into a career

Level	Pre-intermediate onwards
Activity type	Groupwork
Equipment/ Materials	Single VHS player and TV
Plus ...	A camcorder and empty boxes (see below)

- Find some fairly anonymous cardboard boxes such as cereal packets or shoe boxes. Cover these completely in white paper, using glue or sticky tape so that labelling is no longer visible. These boxes will be the dummy products your class will sell.

- Watch some TV commercials with the class, preferably in English. Discuss the strategies used in the different advertisements.

- Divide the class into groups of four or five. Give each group one of the covered boxes. Tell them that these boxes contain the product they are going to sell.

- Explain that they have to:

  1. decide what the packet contains
  2. decide on its unique selling point
  3. decorate the packet
  4. design, script and film a TV commercial for that product.

- In a corner of the classroom set up a 'studio' and a booking form. When the groups are ready they can book the studio for a slot.

- The class views the advertisements and discusses whether they work.

Appendix

Full set of Example Cards for **Circles (Section 8)**

Summaries Circle

my last holiday	a film I enjoyed
my home	my hobbies
my oldest and dearest friend	my taste in clothes
my hopes for the future	my career
my mother/my father	my pet hates
my family	
my country	
my home town	
a book I enjoyed	

Auxiliary Circle

I'm in my 20s.

I'll be here this time next year.

I've got a car.

I've been to Paris.

I like Chinese food.

I had a good weekend.

I'm enjoying this lesson.

I was late this morning.

I'm wearing my best pair of jeans.

I was talking when the teacher walked in.

I can drive.

I'd like to go to Disneyland.

I can swim.

I used to smoke.

I'm going to do my homework tonight.

I'm going to the cinema tonight.

Reporting Circle (Lower)

<table>
<tr><td>

1
I like ice cream.

</td></tr>
</table>

<table>
<tr><td>

2
**I'm going to
watch TV tonight.**

</td></tr>
</table>

<table>
<tr><td>

3
I've been to Britain.

</td></tr>
</table>

<table>
<tr><td>

4
I can drive.

</td></tr>
</table>

<table>
<tr><td>

5
**Get out and
don't come back!**

</td></tr>
</table>

<table>
<tr><td>

6
What's your name?

</td></tr>
</table>

<table>
<tr><td>

7
Where do you live?

</td></tr>
</table>

<table>
<tr><td>

8
Do you like cooking?

</td></tr>
</table>

<table>
<tr><td>

9
Can you swim?

</td></tr>
</table>

<table>
<tr><td>

10
**Could you help me
with this?**

</td></tr>
</table>

Key

1	She	told me said ~~me~~	(that) she liked ice-cream.
2	She	told me said ~~me~~	(that) she was going to watch TV.
3	She	told me said ~~me~~	(that) she had been to Britain.
4	She	told me said ~~me~~	(that) she could drive.
5	She	told me ~~said~~ *(order)*	to get out and not to come back.
6	She	asked (me)	what my name was.
7	She	asked (me)	where I lived.
8	She	asked (me)	if I liked cooking. whether
9	She	asked (me)	if I could swim. whether
10	She	asked me *(request)*	to help her.

91

Reporting Circle (Upper)

	Key
1 Get out and don't come back!	1 tell/order
2 If I were you, I'd take it back to the shop.	2 advise
3 Don't forget you haven't paid your bill!	3 remind
4 Go on, go to Spain. You'll have a great time!	4 encourage
5 Why don't you come round for dinner?	5 invite

— (someone) to do

6 You ate that chocolate, didn't you!	6 accuse (someone) of
7 I did it. I took the money.	7 admit
8 Don't look at me. I didn't take your pen!	8 deny
9 I'm really sorry but I've broken your watch.	9 apologise for

— doing

Reporting Circle (Upper continued)

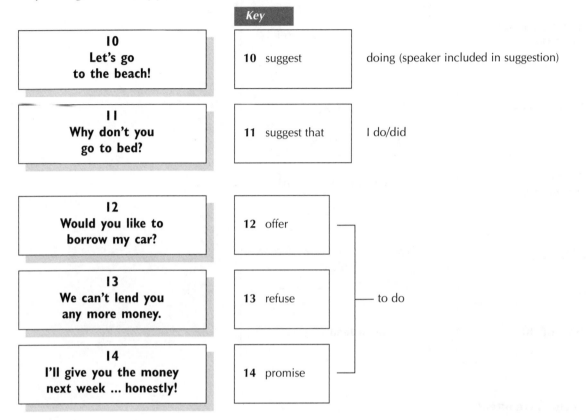

10
**Let's go
to the beach!**

Key

10 suggest   doing (speaker included in suggestion)

11
**Why don't you
go to bed?**

11 suggest that   I do/did

12
**Would you like to
borrow my car?**

12 offer

13
**We can't lend you
any more money.**

13 refuse   — to do

14
**I'll give you the money
next week ... honestly!**

14 promise

Quickfire Circle

What time do you call this?	**You're nicked, mate!**
Where to, guv?	**Alright?**
What seems to be the matter?	**Nice weather for it!**
What do you fancy?	**Warm for the time of year, isn't it?**
Got a light?	**Get a load of that!**
Do you come here often?	
It's my shout.	
What're you having?	
Anything you say may be taken down	

professional
perspectives

professional perspectives is a series of practical methodology books designed to provide teachers of English with fresh insights, innovative ideas and original classroom materials. It is published by DELTA PUBLISHING.

Other titles in the series include:

Creating Conversation in Class
by Chris Sion
More than 100 imaginative ideas and stimulating activities designed to get students talking in class

Humanising your Coursebook
by Mario Rinvolucri
A wide range of activities designed to extend typical coursebook language practice by engaging students creatively and productively

The MINIMAX Teacher
by Jon Taylor
Practical, easy-to-use activities that generate the maximum student output from the minimum teacher input

Using the Mother Tongue
by Sheelagh Deller and Mario Rinvolucri
Ready-to-use activities which make creative use of the students' mother tongue in the language learning classroom

For a full list and further details of titles in the *professional perspectives* series, contact the publishers at:

DELTA PUBLISHING
Quince Cottage
Hoe Lane
Peaslake
Surrey GU5 9SW
England

Tel +44 (0)1306 731770
E-mail info@deltapublishing.co.uk
Web www.deltapublishing.co.uk